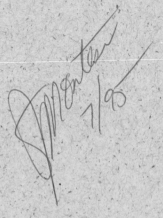

D1416874

Distributed By:
WORLD FUTURE SOCIETY
7910 Woodmont Avenue, Suite 450
Bethesda, Maryland 20814 U.S.A.
For A Free Catalog, Call: 1-800-989-8274

Innovate!

Straight Path to Quality,
Customer Delight,
and Competitive Advantage

Paul A. Schumann, Jr.

Donna C. L. Prestwood

Alvin H. Tong

John H. Vanston

McGraw-Hill, Inc.

New York   San Francisco   Washington, D.C.   Auckland   Bogotá
Caracas   Lisbon   London   Madrid   Mexico City   Milan
Montreal   New Delhi   San Juan   Singapore
Sydney   Tokyo   Toronto

Library of Congress Cataloging-in-Publication Data

Schumann, Paul A.
    Innovate! : straight path to quality, customer delight &
competitive advantage / by Paul A. Schumann, Jr. ... [et al.]
        p.   cm.
    Includes index.
    ISBN 0-07-055714-4
    1. Technological innovations—Economic aspects.   2. Marketing.
3. Competition.   4. Consumer satisfaction.   I. Schumann, Paul A.
HC79.T415455   1994
658.8—dc20   94-7531
                                                                      CIP

1 2 3 4 5 6 7 8 9 0   DOC/DOC   9 0 9 8 7 6 5 4

ISBN 0-07-055714-4

The sponsoring editor for this book was James H. Bessent, Jr., the editing
supervisor was Caroline R. Levine, and the production supervisor was
Suzanne W. Babeuf. This book was set in Palatino by McGraw-Hill's
Professional Book Group composition unit.

Printed and bound by R. R. Donnelley & Sons Company.

This book is printed on recycled, acid-free paper con-
taining a minimum of 50% recycled de-inked fiber.

We dedicate this book to our parents, whom we chose to believe.

D. C. L. P.

P. A. S.

Contents

Preface

Peter Drucker has written, "Business has only two basic functions: marketing and innovation. Marketing and innovation produce results. All the rest are costs."[*] We go even further to state that innovation in *marketing* is also essential. Therefore business has only one basic function—innovation. Innovation is the basis of all competitive advantage: the means by which organizations anticipate and fill customer needs and the method by which organizations utilize technology.

Innovation either endows resources with a new capacity to create wealth or creates a new resource. Innovation is the process of implementing new ideas, of turning creative concepts into realities. In a broader sense innovation can occur in all areas:

- Technical
- Social
- Political
- Economic

Innovation in one area always affects the other areas. Innovation can cause change or it can exploit change; systematic innovation which exploits change is generally the most effective.

Drucker has defined systematic innovation as "the purposeful and organized search for changes, and in the systematic analysis of the opportunities such changes might offer for economic or social innova-

---

[*]Peter F. Drucker, *Innovation and Entrepreneurship*, Harper & Row, New York, (1985).

tion."[*] This book develops a process to implement systematic innovation in organizations.

Organizations need innovation to

- Stay in business

- Delight customers

- Establish competitive advantage

- Deliver quality products and services

- Be more productive

- Meet business goals

- Attract and keep the best people

The purpose of this book is to help the reader create an effective and efficient organization through market-driven, purposeful innovation. The book describes a systematic process of identifying the changes occurring in a market, understanding the opportunities and threats that will result from these changes, developing a strategy to take advantage of the opportunity and avoiding or minimizing threats, assessing the organization's capability to implement the strategy, and developing an organization which can effectively and efficiently innovate.

This book will benefit the reader by introducing him or her to a new way of thinking about organization and innovation. The reader will benefit by learning some new concepts about management which will, when applied appropriately, establish him or her as a leader of organizational change.

The organization will benefit by becoming market driven. It will do what is appropriate for the market and it will anticipate the market. As a result, the organization will become more effective and efficient. The process described in this book will enable organizations to implement the "new business philosophy" described by Drucker in a recent *Wall Street Journal* article. Society will benefit because the organizations within it that create wealth and meet societal needs will be more sharply focused on the proper targets.

The purpose of business is innovation, which, when properly focused, creates wealth as defined in the broadest sense. The creation of wealth benefits all.

[*]Ibid.

We have chosen in our business to help organizations capitalize on change by applying the methodologies of this book in a variety of different settings and applications. We do consulting, facilitation, research, and training to help organizations and their leaders in the "glocal" (global and local simultaneously) marketplace.

Donna C. L. Prestwood
Paul A. Schumann, Jr.
P. O. Box 26947
Austin, Texas 78755
(512) 345-1858 (tel.)
(512) 345-1065 (fax)

Acknowledgments

As is the case in the development of any series of concepts over the years, there are many people too numerous to mention who have listened to and interacted with us on our particular view of organizational innovation. We have given informal talks, formal lectures, seminars, and education programs on portions of as well as all the concepts. And, early on in the development of our perspective on market-driven innovation, we had the great fortune to work with very special people, representing both industry and government institutions, who took the personal risks that allowed us to test the new methodology.

We are highly appreciative of the support and trust that was shown in those early days from several IBMers (past and present), in particular, Robert Doyna, Dennis Rea, and Sam Zigrossi in Austin, Texas; and Gerri Young from the Santa Teresa, California laboratory. We are equally indebted to Drs. Rich Newell and Henrich Bantli of 3M in St. Paul, Minnesota. They early on saw the value of the methodology.

From the government and nonprofit arena, Helen Salter of the NSA, and Ron Edelstein and Ken Kazmer of the Gas Research Institute, were early supporters of the innovation methodology to their specific areas.

We cannot forget the patience of our friends and colleagues. Both Margaret Lehning and Peter Zandan spent untold hours in discussion and discovery with us.

In more recent applications, we are grateful for the support afforded us by some insightful and exuberant people who all wished to make a difference in their respective organizations. Alan Graham, president of the Trilogy Group in Austin, Texas, and Don Van Stone, president of the Austin–San Antonio Corridor Council in San Marcos, Texas, are two we cannot thank enough. We also hold very dear the more recent interactions we have had with people in two very special organizations: Dr. Connie Campbell and Ms. Elaine Munschein of the Learning Exchange; and Ed Weaver and Bob Rogers of the Kauffman Foundation of Kansas City, Missouri. The specific application of these concepts to their particular business was enlightening and greatly beneficial to all involved.

A book like this never happens unless there are many, many hands in the background making things happen. We are especially beholden to our assistant, Catherine Chang. Without her this book would have been virtually impossible. Her good humor, effectiveness, and efficiency in accomplishing all tasks thrown her way are a marvel to behold. She supports us completely while also completing her undergraduate work in international business at the University of Texas. The business world will benefit greatly from Catherine's presence.

1
Purposeful Innovation

The Key to Sustained Competitive Advantage

Exploit Change through Innovation

It is obvious now even to the casual observer that we are in a time in which continuous innovation—a constant commitment to change—is an essential ingredient to organizational success and, even more fundamentally, to survival. Change will never go away. It will always be with us. However, at this moment the pace and magnitude of change is at a crest. In the aftermath of the crest, some of us will be among the missing, swept away by the crosscurrents of change—and this applies to individuals, companies, and whole industries. No one is safe; history teaches us that.

The question, then, is not *whether* to innovate, but *how?* Books and articles by the thousands promise easy solutions or easy strategies. But, as someone once said, for every complex problem there is a simple answer, and it's probably wrong. If we are to solve the problem of continuous organizational innovation, we must respect the complexity of the issue.

Peter Drucker (1985)[1] has written,

> Business has only two basic functions: Marketing and innovation. Marketing and innovation produce results. All the rest are costs.

We believe that innovation in marketing is also essential. Therefore business has only one basic function—innovation. Innovation is the basis of all competitive advantage, the means by which organizations anticipate and fill customer needs, and the method by which organizations utilize technology.

Innovation endows resources with a new capacity to create wealth or creates a new resource. Innovation is the organization's way of implementing new ideas, of turning the creative concepts of its members into realities. It can cause change or it can exploit change. Systematic innovation which exploits change is generally the most effective.

In the American culture, exploiting change is not what is expected of an innovator. America's image of innovators is that of lone inventors struggling against tremendous odds to bring ideas to the world. Then, when they have succeeded, the world rewards them by beating a path to their door. However, this is the least successful way to innovate.

Quite often, the Japanese are labeled as being noninnovative. However, they are very innovative. It is just that they prefer to take advantage of change. When innovations result from change, they seem to be very normal and natural developments, even though they may, in reality, be breakthroughs, such as the Sony Walkman.

Drucker[2] has defined systematic innovation as

> the purposeful and organized search for changes, and in the systematic analysis of the opportunities such changes might offer for economic or social innovation.

This book develops a process to implement systematic innovation in organizations.

Organizations need innovation to

- Stay in business
- Delight customers
- Establish competitive advantage
- Deliver quality products and services
- Be more productive
- Meet goals
- Attract and keep the best people

But how do organizations innovate purposefully, taking advantage of changes that are occurring? Cookbook approaches do not provide the answers. Such approaches are more like a development process, steps to go through in a very general sense, but with little clue as to how to focus the organization's innovative activity.

General advice books are good for hints about creating an innovative culture or organizing for innovation, but they, too, are unfocused. Organizations that follow their advice may well work on unnecessary innovations while forsaking the necessary ones.

And, lastly, the single-strategy books and articles promise success if you just follow their advice. Most of them recommend that you move quickly and that you make incremental changes. This may be good advice for some industries and for certain companies within those industries, but it is not correct for everyone and may lead to failure.

Become Market Driven

The correct strategy is to be market driven; that is, to innovate in the direction the market indicates. This way, the organization can develop the purposeful and organized search for changes that Drucker suggests. The principles of being market driven are very simple, fundamentally sound, and very powerful. To be market driven, organizations must understand the markets, commit to leadership in the markets they choose to serve, execute with excellence across the organization, and keep the customer foremost (Figure 1-1).

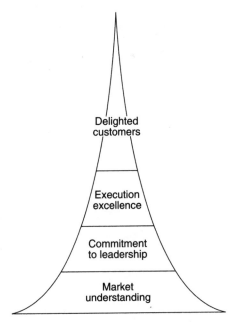

Figure 1-1. Market-driven principles.

What Is a Market?

A market consists of three components: customers, competition, and technology. The pull of the market comes from current, identified potential, and unidentified potential customers. Market push comes from the technology—direct, supportive, and enabling. The clash in the marketplace comes from competitors—direct, indirect, and structural.

A systematic search through these elements of the market identifies the innovation opportunity. Ideally, organizations would prefer to pinpoint an area where customers want innovation, where the technology has the potential to provide it, and where there is little competition. To understand the market, then, is to develop a description of the innovation opportunity. That opportunity is there for everyone to discover. Whether the organization takes advantage of it or not depends on its strategy and capability.

Innovative Organizations

A shared vision is the enabling force that drives an organization. If this vision encompasses the commitment to leadership and embraces innovation, it can be used to develop an innovation strategy; to do that, the innovation opportunity must be developed through understanding the markets. It is through a management style called *teleocracy*, described by Mobley and McKeown (1989),[3] that the vision can be established.

Organizations have gone through three fundamental styles of management over time—autocracy, bureaucracy, and entrepreneurship (or intrapreneurship). Each has its place in history, its organization, and environmental conditions. In the current environment, teleocracy is more appropriate for most organizations.

References

1. Peter F. Drucker, *Innovation and Entrepreneurship*, Harper & Row, New York, 1985.

2. Ibid.

3. Lou Mobley and Kate McKeown, *Beyond IBM*, McGraw-Hill, New York, 1989.

2
Innovative Organizations

A Tradition of the Culture

The Age of Innovation

This is the age of innovation. The world is being altered, at this very moment, by driving forces for change. The economy, massive social and political upheaval, demography, technology, the global market, and developments in organizational science are all encouraging innovation, which is the response to change. (And, conversely, change is the consequence of innovation.) As a result, we are in a time of rapid, revolutionary change. Organizations must anticipate this and innovate in ways that allow them to take advantage of change. An organization's culture is the ultimate governor of the amount and type of innovation that will take place. The organization therefore must have a way to link its culture to its market.

Today changes are being brought about by a set of technologies on which the next economy will be based. The first economic revolution, or wave, was based on agriculture, and the second on industry. The third, or postindustrial, wave will be based on information technologies. The driving technologies of this postindustrial period will be computers, communications and related information technologies, biotechnology, and materials science.

The business opportunity that exists for the "informatization" of the global economy is formidable. *Informatization* is the process of bringing information technologies to all aspects of business, government, and society: computers and advanced communication technology will permeate the home, office, and factory floor. Of course, this opportunity has attracted considerable attention not only from companies in the United States and Japan, but the entire world. This competitive pressure, along with the differing technological approaches of the competitors, has spurred change at an accelerated rate.

Many technologies are now competing to provide solutions to the same problems. In information management, products based on computers and terminals, telephone, and television are all attempting to solve the same problem. And, within a technological approach like television, there are competing supporting technologies—broadcast, direct satellite narrowcast, fiber optics, coaxial cable, and microwave. Hybrid systems involving these technologies are also developing, for example, videotext, which merges computers, telephone, and television.

Innovation does not usually follow linear patterns of development. It quite often lurches ahead by fits and starts from a wide variety of bases. Communication—in the past, in the form of the written word in technical papers, reports, and books—provided the asynchronous means for information to flow from one person to another fueling innovation. Thomas (1974),[1] quoting Ziman, states,

> The technique of soliciting many modest contributions to the store of human knowledge has been the secret of Western science since the 17th Century, for it achieves a corporate, collective power that is far greater than an individual can exert.

Changes in communication capabilities will accelerate the flow of the information that is required for innovation, thereby fostering a burst of innovative actions. Innovation will reach a peak level never before experienced.

At the same time that all this innovation is occurring, society has begun to recognize a need to change the way it thinks about organizations. Rosabeth Moss Kanter (1983),[2] in her landmark book has shown that individual involvement and empowerment is the key to mastering change. Segmentalism must be replaced by integrative approaches. The industrial model of a hierarchical structure—breaking a job down into smaller and smaller pieces so that each individual works on only a small piece—is giving way to what Toffler (1980)[3] called "adhocracies." Temporary structures, task forces, work groups, and the like, which eliminate organizational barriers, are becoming more the norm. Individuals who can work within an organizational structure but form temporary alliances to get the job done are highly valued. Quality circles and quality function deployment (QFD) teams are examples of such alliances within an organizational structure; they attempt to tap the collective and individual knowledge of the workers. Senge (1990)[4] has combined these concepts with others to suggest a "learning organization."

In the current environment, competition has also increased. We are on the verge of having a true worldwide market, in which every organization will have to adopt both a global and local perspective. In today's environment even small organizations, who may think that they serve only a local market, are really competing globally. Therefore the organizational perspective of today should be "glocal." Glocal organizations have a simultaneously global and local viewpoint.

The corporate world has become even more complex than it was—too complex for autocratic management and too fast changing for a bureaucracy. Individual involvement in creative efforts, innovation, and decisions is required. Teleocratic management is emerging as the management technique of the 1990s.

The Challenge to Organizations

The major challenge to every organization today is the transformation of its culture so that the organization can endure and grow through the current revolution. No one is safe. Many strong, good companies existed before the last major revolution in the 1930s; not many survived, and of those that did, few are still at the top.

Von Fange (1959)[5] states in *Professional Creativity* that

> to make creative contributions, as Einstein indicated, requires that one always search for what is fundamental. Or, to phrase it another way, if buggy-whip people had realized that they were not in the business of making high-quality buggy whips, but rather in the business, fundamentally, of stimulating further output from the prime mover of the family conveyance, their factories would not now be gaunt skeletons upon the American industrial scene.

T. J. Watson, Jr., (1963)[6] observed in *A Business and Its Beliefs,*

> Technological change demands an even greater measure of adaptability and versatility of the management in a large organization. Unless management remains alert, it can be stricken with complacency—one of the most insidious dangers we face in the business. In most cases, it's hard to tell that you've even caught the disease until it's almost too late. It is frequently most infectious among companies who have reached the top. They get to believing in the infallibility of their own judgments.

Watson further states,

Of the top 25 industrial corporations in the United States in 1900, only two remain in that select company today. One retains its original identity; the other is a merger of seven corporations on that original list. Two of those 25 failed. Three others merged and dropped behind. The remaining 12 have continued in business, but each has fallen substantially in its standing. Figures like these help to remind us that corporations are expendable and that success—at best—is an impermanent achievement that can always slip out of hand.

Despite these warnings, the company founded by Watson's father and guided by the son to greatness, IBM, has had the very thing he warned about happen. IBM developed a business model which was very successful in the environment of the past. The environment shifted, driven by social, political, economic, and demographic forces for change. Customer needs, technological capability, and competitive responses changed. As a result, the IBM business model, once the paragon of success, failed; IBM is now having to develop a new business model and is losing money at a prodigious rate while it changes. The challenge is to be able to anticipate the shifts and change the organization constructively instead of waiting for the problems to get so large that only destructive change is possible.

The Organization's Response

Everyone in an organization must be innovative; that is the only way that the organization will be able to change fast enough to meet the demands of its customers, stay technologically competent, effectively deal with competition, and respond to the pressures of change both from within and without.

To allow each person in the organization to be innovative, the organization must have a broad definition of *innovation,* one that encompasses all members of the organization and each of its functional subunits. This definition must be able to transcend organizational structures and be useful to every functional subunit, from marketing through research to development to manufacturing.

Members of the organization at all levels must be able to communicate effectively with each other about innovation. It would be helpful if the method of communication broke down stereotypical thinking patterns, if it put innovation into a new context so old methods of thinking could not be used and personal issues could not surface. These kinds of results can be accomplished with an *innovation map.*

The innovation map we have found to be most useful shows nine

	Class		
Nature	Incremental	Distinctive	Breakthrough
Product			
Process			
Procedure			

Figure 2-1. Innovation map.

different types of innovation (Figure 2-1). Along one axis is displayed the nature of the innovation. The other axis shows the class of the innovation. The *nature* of the innovation is classified into one of three categories:

- *Product* innovations are those involving the function provided to customers (external or internal) or the form that function takes. Examples include improvements in industrial machinery, consumer goods, software, and component parts. The product can also be a service, such as next-day package delivery. Product innovations involve the way things interact with things.

- *Process* innovations are those that involve the way a product is developed, produced, and provided. Examples include improvements in manufacturing processes, distribution systems, and the development of CAD/CAM. Process innovations involve the interaction of people with things.

- *Procedure* innovations are those that involve the way in which products and processes are integrated into the operations of the organization. Examples include improvements in marketing methods, administrative methods, sales terms and conditions, and requirements generation. Procedure innovations involve the way people interact with people.

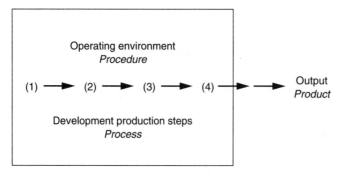

Figure 2-2. The nature of innovation.

As shown in Figure 2-2, changes in the output are product innovations, changes in production steps are process innovations, and changes in the operating environment are procedure innovations. For example, at the corporate level of General Motors, automobiles are products, production methods are processes, and marketing tactics are procedures.

Note that this classification system emphasizes the fact that the term *innovation* does not apply only to hard technologies, but also to new procedures, standards, or approaches. Also note that this classification approach can be used in different parts of the organization. For example, in the planning department of General Motors, the annual business plan could be a product, the methods used to develop the plan could be a process, and the way the plan is coordinated could be a procedure.

The second dimension of the classification structure—the *class* of innovation—indicates how great a change from present practice the innovation represents (see Figure 2-3).

- *Incremental* innovations are those that reflect a relatively small improvement over present products, processes, and procedures. These are advances that are a little better, a little faster, or a little cheaper.

- *Distinctive* innovations are those that provide significant advances or improvements, but are not based on fundamentally new technologies or approaches.

- *Breakthrough* innovations are those that are based on fundamentally different technologies and approaches, and that allow the performance of functions that were previously not possible, or the performance of presently possible functions in a manner that is strikingly superior to the old. Breakthrough innovations result in a significant

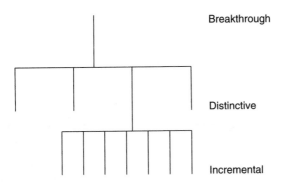

Figure 2-3. The class of innovation.

number of distinctive innovations, and these, in turn, result in a flood of incremental innovations.

A breakthrough innovation results in the creation of a new industry or class of technologies—the creation of a new set or cluster of subsequent, less significant distinctive innovations. A distinctive innovation is the creation of a new member in the set initiated by a breakthrough innovation. Incremental innovations result in changes to distinctive innovations.

At the societal level, the development of the incandescent light was a breakthrough innovation. The changes from carbon filaments to metal filaments and from evacuated bulbs to gas-filled bulbs were distinctive innovations. The development of methods to produce the bulbs more quickly, more reliably, and less expensively were incremental innovations. Likewise, the discovery of superconductivity was a breakthrough innovation. Development of superconducting wires was a distinctive innovation. Development of manufacturing processes to produce superconducting magnets commercially was incremental. The recent discovery of high-temperature superconductors was, on the other hand, another breakthrough innovation.

As with the nature of innovation, the class of innovation may vary with the industry, company, or subordinate organizational unit. For example, an innovation that might be breakthrough on a Honda production line could be distinctive at the manufacturing division level, and incremental at corporate headquarters.

The utility of these two classification schemes is sharply increased when they are combined to form the two-dimensional matrix of the innovation map. The map can be used in a variety of ways to help organizations, and the level of application can vary from specific innovation prospects, to competing (intraorganizational) innovation solutions, to

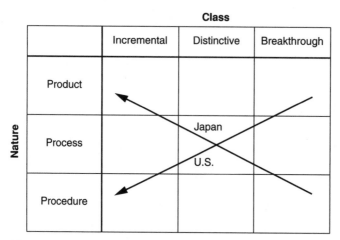

Figure 2-4. Patterns of innovation for three-dimensional integrated circuit development.

comparisons of companies, industries, or countries. It is also quite useful in areas such as technology transfer and technology fusion.

For example, the innovation map was used in 1988, in an analysis of differences in innovation patterns between the U.S. and Japanese microelectronics industry. Figure 2-4 shows the resulting innovation patterns for three-dimensional integrated-circuit development. The arrows indicate that the United States tends to start with breakthrough product innovation, then develop process and procedure support structures. On the other hand, Japan tends to start with breakthrough procedural support structures, then move to developing process and product innovations.

Everyone within an organization can and should innovate in one or more areas in this map. The innovation map is a very useful tool for discussions with individuals and groups about innovations and their goals; it can also be used as a creativity enhancement tool.

The innovation map is useful to depict the focus of the innovation enhancement programs that the organization either has in place or is considering. Analysis of the map will provide significant insight regarding the appropriateness of the program and its potential value to the organization.

Figure 2-5 depicts the innovation focus of several of the traditional types of organizational programs. It should be noted that in many instances an organization can make a serious mistake in implementation because of failures explicitly to understand or accurately to predict the potential results of one or more programs. It is not enough to

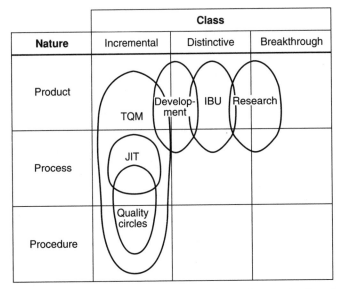

Figure 2-5. Depiction of several traditional organizational programs in an innovation map. In this figure IBU stands for *independent business unit*, TQM is *total quality management*, and JIT stands for *just in time*.

have innovation programs; these programs should meet the innovation needs of the marketplace, and the innovation map is the tool that can be effectively used to match market needs with organizational programs. Therefore, the innovation map is most useful when part of a structured approach for developing and implementing an effective innovation program.

Paradigms

Organizational innovation capability is limited by the way in which the organization views the world. All organizations operate within paradigms. Paradigms provide filters and models that allow certain information to penetrate the consciousness of the organization while repelling other types of information. Paradigms control the amount of innovation in an organization, as well as its focus.

Thomas Kuhn (1970)[7] introduced the concept of paradigms to describe how technical and social progress occurs. A *paradigm* is an example, coming from the Greek *paradigma*. Current usage has broadened its definition, however, to mean a pattern, a set of rules, proce-

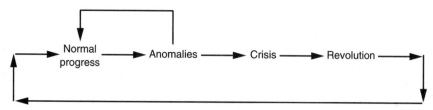

Figure 2-6. Progress and paradigm development.

dures, beliefs, values, perceptions, standards, and theories. In the context of an organization, it's "the way things are done."

The process of technical change described by Kuhn is shown in Figure 2-6. During normal progress, the paradigm is well established. The rules are understood. Theories have been tested. Progress occurs by puzzle solving. Rules and procedures are used to solve problems for which solutions are assumed to exist, and it is assumed that the tools being used will apply to the problem. Motivation comes from the clever application of the rules.

Occasionally, anomalies occur. Sometimes these are minor, and slight changes to the paradigm result in progress. Generally, however, the anomalies begin to pile up. They are put away for future consideration. At this juncture, the individual assumes that he or she is not smart enough to apply the paradigm to the problem; the unsolved problems are shelved, awaiting more knowledge or better instruments.

A crisis occurs whenever the weight of the unsolved problems has built up to the point that they can no longer be ignored. Reluctantly, attention is turned to the pile of unresolved issues. Or sometimes a destructive anomaly is discovered that irrevocably destroys the old paradigm.

Even as all of this transpires, a revolution does not occur unless there is a new paradigm available. When there is a new paradigm, at first only a few people begin to adopt it. Progress is slow—only after some amount of time passes, usually measured in years or decades, does a transition take place from the old paradigm to the new. Once evidence of the new paradigm's capabilities becomes strong enough, things start to happen quickly.

In the case of technical progress, years of experience in developing knowledge in the old paradigms is negated, and careers altered or stopped. For businesses, obsolescence becomes a problem and large amounts of money are lost. This is what is occurring worldwide today: Large organizations, businesses, and political institutions have found that their paradigms, the ones that were in the past so successful, have now reached their limits and that in order to succeed in a global environment, significant restructuring of the organization must occur.

In organizations, a similar process occurs. When a paradigm is well established, everyone knows what to work on, how to approach problems, and the range of acceptable answers. The organization has a purpose, and, if the paradigm is strong, everyone knows how they fit into that purpose. When anomalies occur in an organization, people may not even know that mistakes are being made. Unlike technical progress, there is often no "physical reality" inside organizations to compare with. The models keep getting used, and people are developing incorrect solutions to problems and even working on the wrong problem. It is only when the product or service of the organization fails to satisfy customers, is no longer competitive, or utilizes completely obsolete technology that years of mistakes appear in one cataclysmic revelation. The organization then awakens abruptly to the need for change, usually long after the change was necessary.

Figure 2-7 indicates how this process takes place. At the first appearance of a new paradigm, a breakthrough innovation, its problem-solving capability is limited. After more is known about how to use the new rules, problem-solving capability increases rapidly as distinctive and incremental innovations are introduced. These are the "glory years" of the paradigm. Nearly every problem that comes along can be solved. Eventually, however, there is saturation, and, once again, large amounts of effort are expended with very little change, and only incremental innovation is left.

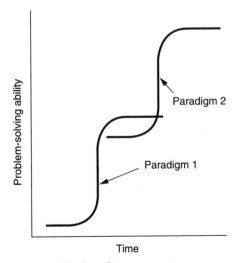

Figure 2-7. Paradigm progress.

The second paradigm has meanwhile already entered the scene. It always has lower problem-solving capability at the beginning than the older paradigm it will replace. Eventually, it surpasses the old paradigm and it too saturates. As organizations switch to the new paradigm during its early stage of development, there is always a step backwards in performance. In the early stages of a new paradigm it takes courage to adopt it and foresight as to the new paradigm's ultimate problem-solving capability.

An organization that, for whatever reasons, fails to make the jump during the early period or opts to "wait and see," runs a risk of extraordinary proportions. The costs of playing catch-up during periods of rapid change are exceedingly high in both monetary and human terms, and the risk is that the organization may never overtake its competitors.

Bacon stated, "Truths emerge more readily from error than from confusion." This notion is crucial to an understanding of the paradox of the paradigm. The anomaly exists only against the background of the paradigm. If the paradigm did not exist, the anomaly would not exist, so the paradigm both enables progress and limits its extent. The rules and procedures are necessary, but their very existence limits progress. Organizations need paradigms to be efficient, but the very existence of the paradigm limits the organization's effectiveness.

The metaphor that would equate technical paradigms to organizational paradigms breaks down at this point. In technical progress, paradigms are used to explain the physical world, which does not change. The limits of paradigms are measured against a fixed physical world that is successfully revealed and explained by new paradigms, and measurements of the physical world are used to test the paradigm. In organizations, the target is constantly shifting. The market is the symbol of the physical world, and it rarely stays the same. As a result, the effects of the saturation of capability of a paradigm and the movement of the market combine to cascade the downfall of the old paradigm, accelerating the rate of change. In addition, where capability merely saturates in technical paradigms when the limits have been reached, in the case of organizations, capability declines.

Organizational Culture

Deal and Kennedy (1982)[8] have shown that organizations that have strong cultures are more successful. They point out that there is really no absolute—no one "correct" culture. Suitability of a particular culture depends on the business the organization is engaged in. Strong-culture organizations perform better than weak-culture ones. The stronger the culture, the smaller the amount of information that must be transmitted in any transaction. A strong culture produces an efficient organization.

Deal and Kennedy identified four characteristics of an organizational culture:

- Values
- Rites and rituals
- Heroes and heroines
- Cultural network

Any program that would attempt to change the organizational culture must reflect changes in all these elements.

An organization's culture reflects the organization's paradigm. Within a paradigm, a focused and strong organizational culture is required for the organization to be effective and efficient. But, the existence of a strong organizational culture ensures the resistance of the organization to change (Figure 2-8).

A strong, market-driven organizational culture focused to produce the type of innovation required by the market is essential to success. However, that culture must have built into it a flexible methodology for change. The culture must have

- A clear and compelling shared vision
- An active, broad innovation enhancement program that addresses the necessary types of innovation and utilizes all the elements of the culture
- Sensitivity to the external environment

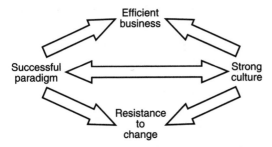

Figure 2-8. Paradigm paradox of organizational culture.

- Strategic planning for the operation, technology, and people
- The broadest concept of the organization's purpose
- Progressive human resource practices that ennoble, enable, empower, and encourage people to develop and grow, build expertise, freely communicate, and have access to the power tools of change
- Integrative management approaches

Through this, a strong corporate culture can be built which will be flexible enough to enable the corporation to meet the challenges of rapid change. If the focus of the culture is market driven, the organization will be effective. If the culture is strong, the organization will be efficient.

Cultural transformation is a strategic planning tool. Cultural transformation is one of the most powerful tools available to move the organization into the position of accepting change and aligning itself with the market. And for those cases where change was not anticipated, a strong but flexible culture will enable a rapid response. Innovation must become a tradition of the culture.

What is needed therefore is a methodology to link the market and the culture of the organization, making it possible for the organization to produce the kind of innovation the market demands, when the market demands it. This book is about a methodology to do just that.

References

1. Lewis Thomas, *The Lives of a Cell,* The Viking Press, New York, 1974.
2. Rosabeth Moss Kanter, *The Change Masters,* Simon & Schuster, New York, 1983.
3. Alvin Toffler, *The Third Wave,* Morrow, New York, 1980.
4. Peter M. Senge, *The Fifth Discipline,* Doubleday Currency, New York, 1990.
5. F. E. Von Fange, *Professional Creativity,* Prentice-Hall, Englewood Cliffs, NJ, 1959.
6. T. J. Watson, Jr., *A Business and Its Beliefs,* McGraw-Hill, New York, 1963.
7. Thomas Kuhn, *The Structure of Scientific Revolutions,* The University of Chicago Press, 1970.
8. Terrence Deal and Allan Kennedy, *Corporate Culture,* Addison-Wesley, Reading, MA, 1982.

3

Market-Driven Innovation

A Systematic Method to Focus and Encourage Innovation

Need to Focus Innovation Efforts

After three decades of "fast second," "stick to your knitting," and "the pursuit of quality" types of organizational philosophies, decision makers have come to realize that continuing innovation is the essential factor for organizational success. Although most organizations now appreciate the importance of innovation to their prosperity, the truth is that few are being very effective and efficient in producing innovation. Targeting innovative efforts is always difficult, and getting the organization's projects, resources, and culture aligned with each other and focused on the market is a formidable task.

Business history is replete with examples of organizations that have expended tremendous efforts on innovation programs that when brought to fruition had little direct value in the marketplace. The failure of Polaroid's "instant movie camera" in competition with video cameras, the limited success of Kodak's disc camera when it had to compete with improved electronic 35mm photography, the ill-fated venture of Exxon into the world of office machines, and Xerox's office automation system illustrate the fact that poorly conceived innovation projects lead to poor results. In fact, the improper focusing of innovation programs can be almost as dangerous to an organization as a "sit still" innovation policy.

19

Polaroid's instant movie camera was an incorrect response to a correctly understood customer need. Where Polaroid failed was in letting the response be driven by internal capability and not understanding competitive response and technological capability. Since they had instant film technology, it was natural for them to build on it. However, video technology was improving too quickly, and the window of opportunity closed before Polaroid could improve instant movie film technology to the point of customer acceptability.

The failure of Kodak's disc camera was slightly different. Again, the market demand for simple, quality photographs was understood. The failure was in the strategy Kodak chose to take advantage of the opportunity. Kodak's primary business is film. Through the disc camera, they were attempting to develop proprietary film technology that would give them an advantage over competitors like Fuji. They also failed to understand the impact of the integration of electronic circuitry onto chips. This made the automatic 35mm camera a reality, bringing a higher-quality image to the mass market.

Exxon's mid-1970s venture into word processors was doomed by a failure in the understanding of the technology. Exxon correctly identified office automation as a significant opportunity. Also, they correctly understood that they shouldn't attempt to develop a product internally. In purchasing Vydec, they misjudged how fast the technology was going to move and what it would take to stay in the game. In addition, the culture of a petroleum company and that of a word processor company are and need to be vastly different. The cultures were too different for the venture to last.

Xerox's first office automation system effort was based on a misjudgment of the time frame of the opportunity. They correctly understood that office automation was a significant opportunity, but they misjudged how fast the opportunity was going to develop. They became technology and innovation driven. They wanted to be advanced and different. As a result, their concepts and technologies were years ahead of the market; many are only just now being utilized by successful companies.

These are all historical examples, but the problems have certainly not gone away. One currently unfolding story is Toyota's latest entry into the pickup truck market. Only 2445 T100s had sold by early 1993, a rate far less than required to meet their 50,000 annual sales projection. Already successful in the small pickup truck market, Toyota apparently could not figure out how to differentiate themselves from their competition in the market for larger pickup trucks. They misunderstood customer needs when they attempted to segment the market into three categories of trucks, and produced an entry in the middle for which there appears to be little or no demand.

On the other hand, many organizations have better understood the overall market and the environmental driving forces and have succeeded by targeting their innovative efforts more effectively. The development of aspartame by the NutraSweet Company, of the Walkman by Sony, and of a truly lap-top computer by Compaq illustrate how product innovations can be successful. The commitment of Motorola, Black & Decker, and Ford to improved production processes has provided each with markedly enhanced competitive positions, while the skyrocketing growth of Dell Computers and Wal-Mart shows that new procedural approaches can also produce impressive results.

The point is that innovation effort is valuable if it is properly targeted. Contrary to the emerging opinion that incremental innovation in manufacturing processes is a panacea for all industries, the truth is that there is no innovation strategy that is appropriate for all companies in all situations. What is needed is a method for effectively analyzing the overall environment in which an organization operates, and for developing an innovation program that matches the needs of the customers, the realities of technological progress, the impact of competition, and the capabilities of the organization.

Innovation in products and services, in processes, and in operational procedures is essential to the success of any organization. Whether the innovation is incremental, distinctive, or breakthrough should be determined by the future needs of the market. Effective targeting must include analysis of developing customer needs, emerging technologies, the total competitive environment, internal capabilities, and basic organizational goals. An efficient organization has both formal and informal mechanisms to properly align these elements and convert the analyses into productive innovation programs.

Current conditions speak volumes to many organizations about the need for change and innovation. For example, Boeing is focusing significant effort on "not doing what IBM, Sears Roebuck, and General Motors have done." The action plan put in place by Boeing is full of process and procedural innovation requirements. The impact of those requirements will be largely incremental. Importantly, the marketplace opportunity points toward the need for distinctive and breakthrough innovation. Boeing will find it difficult to avoid doing the very things it publicly states it does not want to do.

A New Approach to Targeting Innovation Efforts

In determining the most appropriate innovation strategy for an organization, a number of factors must be considered:

1. What is the time frame the organization considers to constitute its initial "window of opportunity"?

2. What is the market the organization chooses to serve? What are the critical driving forces for change affecting the marketplace?

3. What are the current and future needs of the customers in the marketplace? Is the market relatively satisfied with present products and services, or is there pent up desire for new capabilities?

4. Who are the real competitors, and what are they doing? Are present competitors stressing small advances, or are they emphasizing more basic changes? What competitive responses can be anticipated to meet the needs of customers? Are new and unexpected competitors emerging?

5. What are the key technologies in the marketplace? Are they mature, developing, or in a state of transition? What are the underlying supportive and enabling technologies? What is their status? Are there any new technologies which could affect the marketplace?

6. What resources are available for innovation efforts? What is the state of the organization's personnel, facilities, funding, intellectual property, and strategic alliances?

7. Who are the stakeholders of the organization? What are their needs, hopes, and desires?

8. What are the long- and short-term objectives of the organization? Does it seek to be on the forward edge of technology and organizational development, or is it more comfortable with a conservative approach?

9. What is the current culture of the organization? What type of change does it permit?

The market-driven innovation methodology is a mechanism to answer all the questions above, plus others, and then to structure the responses in such a way that informed decisions can be made. The result is a creative and productive, purposeful and flexible innovation program. Application of this methodology is divided into four separate but coordinated tasks (Figure 3-1).

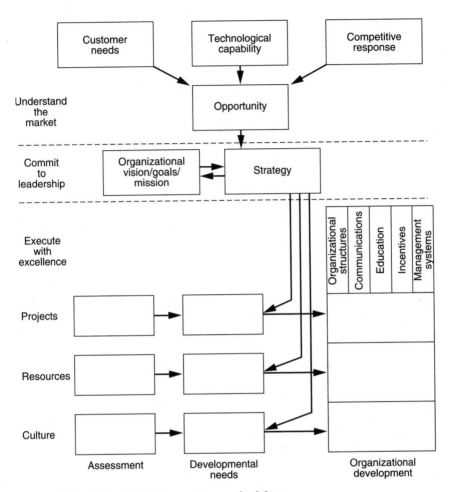

Figure 3-1. Market-driven innovation methodology.

It is best to follow the logic of the tasks presented. However, special situations and requirements often demand that these tasks be done in some other order. Regardless, if all the tasks are fulfilled, sufficient information will be obtained to complete the innovation analysis. There are four basic tasks in the market-driven innovation methodology:

- Understand the market
- Commit to leadership
- Execute with excellence
- Keep customers foremost

Understand the Market

To understand the market means to develop a clear perspective on its future threats and opportunities. The first step in this task is to decide on the time frame of the initial window of opportunity. The early estimate may be refined as more information is developed, but it is useful on the first pass to start with a longer time frame than may be ultimately needed. Next, a clear definition of the market the organization chooses to serve should be developed, and the critical driving forces for change affecting the marketplace assessed. The organization then develops an understanding of current and potential customers in the market. The current and future needs of the customers are then determined. Finally, customer satisfaction with present products and services is determined.

The organization must then assess its competition, how they may respond to future customer needs and how they may be affected by the driving forces for change.

Lastly, the organization should assess technology. First the key technologies in the marketplace are ascertained. It is determined if they are mature, developing, or in a state of transition. The capabilities of these technologies to meet the needs of the marketplace are then verified. Finally, new technologies are reviewed for possible inclusion.

When all this information is gathered, an evaluation can be made of the threats and opportunities in the market over time.

Commit to Leadership

A leader in a market is an organization that establishes the ground rules by which all the competitors have to play. To commit to leadership means to seek out the way in which the organization can exploit the opportunity in the market while minimizing or avoiding the threats, meet the needs of its stakeholders, satisfy its business objectives, and effectively and efficiently utilize its own capabilities. A strategy is the organization's way to interpret the market and accomplish leadership.

Execute with Excellence

To execute with excellence means to have an accurate understanding of the organization's capability, understand the differences between the organization's capabilities and the needs of the strategy, and to commit to the development of the organization so that it can effectively and efficiently execute the strategy. This requires a long-term commitment to the organization's projects, resources (including people), and culture. It means treating the organization as a renewable resource, not an expendable one.

For most organizations, the development of the culture is the controlling element. But whichever element—projects, resources, or culture—controls the development of the organization, that element determines the minimum strategic time frame that must be chosen for the analysis. For example, if changing the culture will require five years, the time frame of the analysis must be at least five years. The time frame can be longer if the market dynamics demand it.

Keep Customers Foremost

Keeping the customer foremost means that throughout the entire market-driven innovation methodology, the customer's needs, current and future, must have the highest priority. Delighting customers results from anticipating their needs, and effectively and efficiently utilizing technology and the organization's capability to fulfill those needs in ways the organization's competitors do not.

Application of Market-Driven Innovation

In each case where the market-driven innovation methodology has been employed significantly, easily observable benefits have resulted. We have found the methodology to be particularly useful in the following areas:

- *Understanding complex and chaotic markets.* One organization, already known for its innovation, used this methodology to understand the emerging market for intelligent vehicle highway systems (IVHS). IVHS is a large, complex market with many systems, subsystems, products, and technologies. IVHS, simply stated, involves the merging of electronics, communication, and computer hardware and software systems to produce "smart" cars, "smart" highways, and the systems that link them together. Using this methodology, it was possible to understand how the market was evolving and for the organization to determine a strategy to enter the market. The methodology provided insights not possible with conventional methods; it also allowed the organization to develop a way to handle the technological changes that must accompany this new market.

- *Developing organizational vitality.* In today's environment organizations must be vital. To be vital means to be alive, growing, developing, changing, and learning. In one case a large software development division of a worldwide corporation used this methodology to determine a strategy to keep its organization vital and identify a set of values that the organization must develop to transcend the software and system changes on the horizon.

- *Creating a vision and a consistent culture.* A presently small commercial real estate firm, The Trilogy Group, whose founder and owner, Alan Graham, has a view of the future that is grand and entrepreneurial, adopted the methodology to completely structure the organization. The methodology was first used to create, then to clarify, the vision, mission, and goals of the organization. Then the entire organization worked together to understand the market, and to develop strategies to take advantage of the identified opportunities. Finally, the organization has begun to plan and develop programs to create consistency in the organizational culture.

- *Creating strategic direction.* The Austin–San Antonio Corridor Council is an economic development organization for a region of Central Texas. This methodology was used in a workshop retreat setting to reestablish the direction of the organization, unify diverse factions that were pulling the organization apart, and establish clear vision, mission, and goals.

- *Applying quality to R&D.* Quality programs have been very successful in some manufacturing organizations, but not very successful in R&D organizations. This methodology was used in the R&D division of a large petrochemical company to structure a measurement system to improve quality and effectiveness.

- *Comparing organizational objectives with actual programs.* Often, in carrying out strategic programs, basic objectives become lost in execution activities. This methodology provides an excellent means of relating the two. For example, at one large, high-tech organization, the management had specifically charged its research and development staff to concentrate on forefront-type innovations. Although there was general agreement in the company that this mandate was being followed, an analysis showed that the bulk of the R&D projects actually underway were of an incremental, short-term type. Moreover, an analysis of the existing incentive program clearly showed why this shift in effort had occurred, as well as how the program should be changed.

- *Facilitating communications between various groups within the organization.* The need to classify technologies, markets, competitive actions, and internal resources requires the establishment of common vocabulary and thought structures, but these are often lacking in large organizations. For example, at a large chemical company using this methodology, research, manufacturing, and marketing people said that, for the first time, they truly understood the objectives and concerns of their counterparts.

- *Identifying future opportunities and threats.* Given this methodology's emphasis on innovation, it is not surprising that it is primarily future oriented. Thus, it tends to look at what the market environment *will be* rather than what it *is*. This orientation has often uncovered opportunities and threats that would otherwise have been overlooked in traditional planning approaches. In an analysis of a large telecommunications company, business opportunities were identified not only in its traditional market area, but also in associated areas of interest.

- *Formulating an innovation enhancement program.* Often, an organization wishes to enhance and expand the innovation activities of its people. A first step in accomplishing this is an analysis of the innovation potential of its employees and of its own innovation environment. A large computer company assessed the innovation propensities of its employees in order to tailor an effective innovation program, and a large government agency conducted a similar assessment. In the latter case, the innovation program will be integrated with a "quality management program."

- *Providing continuity of planning and execution between organizational levels.* The market-driven innovation methodology and its vocabulary are basically the same at all organizational levels. Hence, efforts can be started at top levels and filtered down, or started at lower levels and aggregated to the corporate level. At the Gas Research Institute, the latter approach was applied. Analysis started with small commercial air-conditioning equipment and extended to the Space Conditioning Division. On the other hand, at the previously mentioned high-tech company, the methodology was started at corporate headquarters and will later be extended to subordinate groups.

- *Assisting people to break out of stereotypical thinking modes.* Most managers and executives spend the bulk of their time solving familiar problems in familiar ways. The special structure of the market-driven innovation methodology forces people to think of situations in new contexts. For example, one organization examined its promotion policies and procedures. Early in the analysis, the organization found, to its surprise, that present policies and procedures were strongly motivating activities that management was trying to discourage.

- *Creating a team.*   In all the examples cited above, and in many others, a team was truly created. Members of different groups within the organization were brought together. During the time they worked together they came to understand and use a common language. Moreover, they developed and shared common purposes and were confidently able to take the output from their efforts and directly create innovative programs.

Long-Term Value of the Market-Driven Innovation Methodology

Over the last decade, executives have been bombarded by a plethora of "slogan solutions" which promise quick fixes to their management problems. Theory Z management, quality circles, the book *The One-Minute Manager*, "management by walking around," and a host of others have each had their day in the sun and have, to a large extent, faded into the dusk. Each of these approaches has had its utility. However, each has addressed only a limited aspect of the organization's operation.

These approaches have drawbacks. They tend to

- Focus on a single element of the organization, while the market-driven innovation methodology deliberately involves all elements.

- Focus on a single level in the organization's chain of responsibility, whereas this methodology can be applied equally well at all levels.

- Focus on a snapshot in time, while this methodology is organized to address a dynamically changing environment over time.

- Not be able to link the organizational culture to market needs, while this methodology allows the organization to link its culture to market needs.

Market-driven innovation is fundamentally different from these other concepts. Although its concept is simple, its effective application requires effort, imagination, and insight. The primary value of the methodology is not an immediate solution to immediate problems.

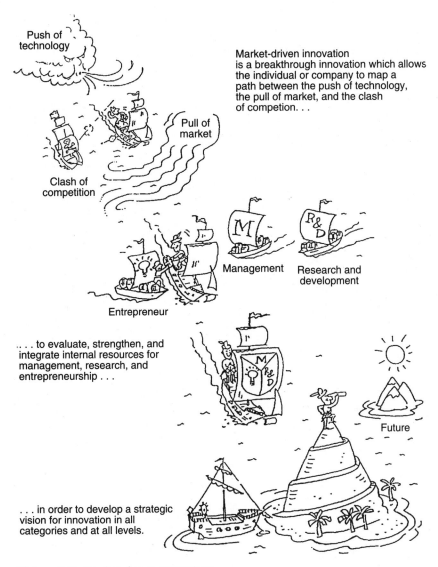

Push of technology

Market-driven innovation is a breakthrough innovation which allows the individual or company to map a path between the push of technology, the pull of market, and the clash of competion. . .

Pull of market

Clash of competition

Management

Research and development

Entrepreneur

.. . . to evaluate, strengthen, and integrate internal resources for management, research, and entrepreneurship . . .

Future

. . . in order to develop a strategic vision for innovation in all categories and at all levels.

Figure 3-2. Market-driven innovation.

Rather, it is an examination of the fundamental structure of the organization, the markets it serves, and the business environment in which it operates. It can act as a generator for a business model which can effectively tie the organization to its environment.

Moreover, the market-driven innovation methodology provides a means for making basic changes in the organization's approach to opportunities and threats. Since the primary focus of this methodology is on innovation, it forces the organization to look to the future—and, most important, it provides the organization with a method for examining and exploiting that future in a logical, structured, sustained manner while maintaining its creativity.

This methodology is not a quick fix to all management problems. It is a method for enhancing and expanding the innovation efforts of the organization and for focusing these efforts to better achieve both long- and short-term organizational goals and objectives. One of the participants in a seminar on the methodology summed up her perspective on the approach with a drawing, which has been recreated in Figure 3-2. She stated that market-driven innovation is a breakthrough innovation which allows the individual or company to map a path between the push of technology, the pull of the market, and the clash of competition, and to evaluate, strengthen, and integrate internal resources for management, research, and entrepreneurship in order to develop a strategic vision for innovation in all categories and at all levels.

4

Discovering the Opportunity in the Market

Defining the Market

A market is composed of three major elements: customers, competition, and technology. Customer needs are anticipated and filled through the use of technology by the organization and its competitors. A market must have, in addition to customers, competition, and technology, a time frame, geographical reference, scale, and scope. In a market, money, goods, services, and/or information are exchanged.

Markets have evolved over time. In its earliest use, *market* referred to a place, usually a juncture between roads where people were likely to meet. In time, markets became more specific places for exchange within towns and villages. However, in today's environment markets are no longer always tied to a concrete locale; instead the term has come more to represent a set of conditions. These conditions generally are descriptions for each of the elements mentioned above. Defining a market is not a linear process.

The market-driven innovation methodology assumes that the organization has at least a vague sense of direction. It assumes that there is an ongoing purpose and that the organization is attempting to make decisions about whether to

- Stay where they are
- Develop new markets

- Develop new products or services
- Diversify
- Integrate their operations either forward or backward in the supplier-customer value chain as shown in Figure 4-1.

The process of understanding a market and discovering the opportunities and threats in a market is integrative. After developing an initial understanding of a market and a strategy which helps the organization take advantage of that opportunity, it is useful to assess the consequences of that strategy on the market:

- How will it affect customer needs?
- How will competition respond?
- How will it affect the development of technology?

After the organization has developed its projects, resources, and culture to produce output, which will have consequences to a market, another assessment of the market's opportunities and threats must be conducted (Figure 4-2).

Driving Forces Affecting the Market

Once an initial definition of the market is created, the next step involves taking a "world view" of the driving forces for change and

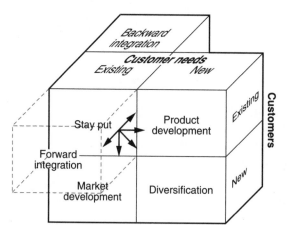

Figure 4-1. Basic strategies for building a business.

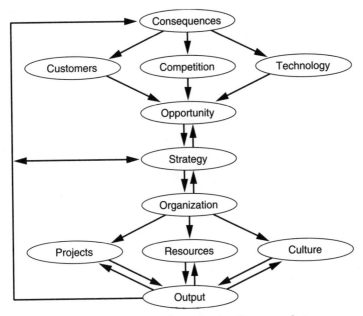

Figure 4-2. Iterative process for understanding a market.

how specific key forces are affecting the current structure and future development of the market. Driving forces for change can be placed in five categories (see Figure 4-3).

Each category is in itself a collection of trends, events, developments, and realities. Each represents a strategic context within which we all live and operate. However, it is the interaction between these categories and their interaction with the market that creates the great force that culminates in change. And, as Figure 4-4 graphically depicts, this change creates needs.

Examples of current driving forces for change at the global level are:

Social: The women's movement
Political: The breakup of the U.S.S.R.
Economic: The continued recession
Demographic: The birth rate in China
Technical: Birth control technologies

It is important to restate that it is the interaction between these categories and in turn their influence upon the market that creates the turbulence and dynamics of the market. And it is crucial to remember

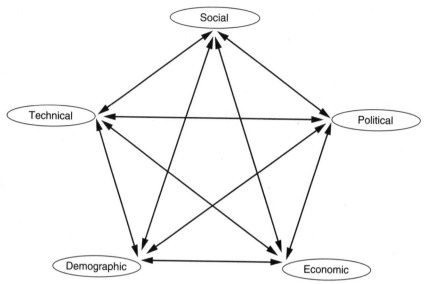

Figure 4-3. Driving forces for change.

that, for all the reasons stated in Chapter 2, this period in history is more turbulent than any other.

Let's bring these forces down from the macro level to the micro level, from global markets to an individual. A Hispanic American male who is 55 years old (demographic), unmarried, the single parent of small children (social), a Republican who voted for Clinton (a Democrat) (political), underemployed (economic), and the owner of a state-of-the-art personal computer with multimedia capabilities (technical) has a different set of needs in many markets than other people. Markets are made up of people who individually and collectively respond to and create driving forces for change. This is why the segmentation of a market is always along one or more of these regions of driving forces for change, and this is also why traditional market research methods, geared to the individual, are usually not useful for assessment of customer needs in the strategic time frame.

What is needed to determine the probable strategic needs of customers, capabilities of technologies, and responses of competition is a methodology to assess the impacts of the driving forces in the market (Figure 4-5). This chapter will describe such a methodology, which has been proven practical by use.

No method can completely predict the future except in "uninteresting" times. In times and markets where little or no change is occurring, or change has been following a predictable pattern, it is easier to

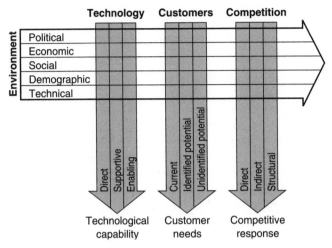

Figure 4-4. Market dynamics.

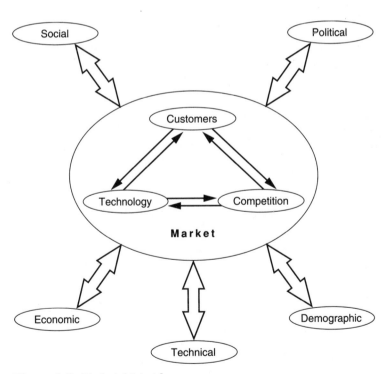

Figure 4-5. Market driving forces.

predict the future. But, in that case, the organization's competitors can also predict the future and it is difficult to establish sustainable competitive advantage.

There is an ancient curse, "May you live in interesting times!" As difficult as life is in interesting times, it is in interesting times that change can be exploited to create or expand markets and to develop significant competitive advantage.

In interesting times, markets are chaotic. *Chaos* describes a state which is not random but which also does not have simple order. The future is always chaotic. There is a higher degree of order in a chaotic market than meets the eye of a casual observer. To determine the probable futures of a market, the organization must develop knowledge of the strong attractors, the interaction of the driving forces for change with each other and customer needs, the technological capabilities, and the competitive responses, around which the future of the market is likely to evolve.

Determination of the driving forces initially is a simple matter:

1. Develop a description of the market.
2. Establish the time frame for the analysis, i.e., five years.
3. List, by category, the driving forces for change that will influence the market you described over the time frame you have identified. Keep in mind that each category must have at least one driving force.
4. Rank each of these forces within its category (social, political, economic, demographic, technical).

If this is a new market for the organization or a market which the organization does not understand, it is advisable to obtain help in determining these driving forces. Information can be obtained by secondary or primary research, calling on expert opinion, using focus groups, or by creating a facilitated team of people within the organization each of whom has partial knowledge.

Who Are the Customers?

Organizations have the tendency, over time, to focus on themselves, their own capabilities, and their own processes. This is especially true if the organization has been successful in the past. They begin to lose contact with customers and begin to trust in their own judgments. This has been exacerbated by the push to shorten the commercialization cycle. Trusting your own judgment is quicker than the messy process of staying in touch with customers. To counter these tendencies, managers are now being encouraged to stay in touch with the customer, or to "listen to the voice of the customer." Many total quality management programs have a large component of customer involvement.

These exhortations to "listen to the customer" are fine if taken in the context of the competition and technology, and the driving forces for change. But the real question is, "Who are the customers?" It does no good to ask "customers" what they want if you don't know who all the customers are.

In fact there are three different types of customers that an organization must contemplate. These three types are most easily considered along the lines of whether they currently purchase from the organization or the organization's competitors. *Current customers* are presently customers of the organization, *identified potential customers* are presently customers of the organization's competitors, and *unidentified potential customers* are presently not customers of either the organization or its competitors.

For the market of fast-food hamburgers, McDonald's has Whitney as a current customer. Donna, her mother, is an identified potential customer, and her grandmother, Louise, is in the unidentified potential customer category. Louise never goes to purchase a fast-food hamburger. Donna prefers a Whataburger. Whitney, incented by the advertisements and toys, always wants to go to McDonald's.

The classification of current, identified potential, and unidentified potential customers is a valuable first pass at segmenting the market. When the organization knows little about the market, this classification system provides a structure that is powerful in focusing its requirements generation process and its marketing efforts.

Segmentation of a market is essential to the success of any business in today's environment. The more that is known about the market, the more refined the segmentation can be and therefore the more targeted the needs and marketing approaches can be. This will be discussed further in Chapter 11.

A simple example of segmentation is the market for faxes. A first impression may be that any business of any size already has a fax. If, however, the classification of customers is combined with a segmentation scheme based on the type of customer, some insights emerge. In Figure 4-6, the X's represent where the primary customers are. In fact, there are some customers in all classifications and types. Most large organizations have already purchased faxes, but there are still some small organizations that have not purchased faxes, and individuals have rarely purchased them for personal use.

This type of analysis obviously provides a way to expand the market for a fax manufacturer. If they only ask questions of their

Type of	Customer classification		
customer	Current	Identified potential	Unidentified potential
Large organizations	X	X	
Small organizations	X	X	X
Individuals			X

Figure 4-6. Simple segmentation of a fax market for a fax manufacturer.

current customers, the organization will only find out how to maintain them as current customers. This is of vital importance to the organization. To not maintain current customers is to lose market share to its competitors. Requirements obtained from the organization's current customers for faxes will more than likely be focused on the problems of current products and services. The organization may also hear about some improvements required. However, it is rare that a current customer will tell the organization about significant changes required.

In general, it is only when competitors have begun to make inroads with the organization's customers that the current customer will be able to describe needs that require distinctive or breakthrough innovations. (There are always rare exceptions, and these are the best type of customers to cultivate, ones who are knowledgeable about a wide variety of direct, indirect, and structural competitors.) Ironically, then, when the organization has done the best job of current customer management, is the time when the organization learns the least from them. A strong base of highly satisfied customers who are looking to no other organization to meet their needs can be a problem. When the knowledge eventually becomes available to them, as it always does, and they reluctantly begin to adopt your competitor's solutions, the changeover is rapid and cataclysmic. By that time, it is too late; the organization has lost its leadership position.

Gathering requirements from the organization's competitors' customers helps. This will give the organization information about what it will take to get these customers to switch from the organization's competitors. Finally, gathering information from the class of customers labeled "unidentified potential" gives the organization information about what it would take to convert a person or organization in this class to a customer. This is likely to require at least a distinctive and possibly a breakthrough innovation.

Figure 4-7. The hierarchy of information.

What Are Their Needs?

The purpose of any method used by an organization should be to help the people in the organization, and therefore the organization itself, to make better decisions. To make better decisions, more or higher-quality information is required. There is a hierarchy of information as represented in Figure 4-7. Organizations are today immersed in a sea of noise, as there is such a proliferation of sources and expansion of those sources' capability to create new information. Without structure and methods to analyze and synthesize all this information, it remains noise. With structure and methods it is possible to develop the information into data that can be used to make decisions. However, even better decisions can be made if knowledge and wisdom can be extracted. These provide the basis for the insights which not only help the organization make better decisions but help it determine what questions to ask. The game is not one of precision but of accuracy. It is far better in today's environment to be approximately correct than to be precisely wrong. The organization must focus on its effectiveness first and then turn its attention to its efficiency.

There are numerous techniques to determine customer needs. Some are focused on the methods of obtaining the data and some are focused on extracting better knowledge from the data. This is not a book on market research techniques; it would require far too much space even to list and describe them all here. What is important for our purposes is to determine which type of technique is best applied to what type of customer so that an accurate innovation map can be developed to satisfy customer needs. Therefore, this section will focus on methods of obtaining the information rather than ways of analyzing and displaying the data.

There are four different types of techniques to determine customer needs. In common usage, these are called *market research techniques*, but as we define the market to be customers, competition, and technology, we will call them *customer needs analysis techniques.* The four types of techniques are

- Surveillance
- Trend analysis
- Expert opinion
- Integrative techniques

Surveillance

Surveillance techniques are based on observation of customers either indirectly, by watching what is being written or said about or by them, or by direct observation of their actions. Scanning, monitoring, and tracking of print media is an excellent way to keep track of what the organization's current customers and identified potential customers are up to and what their needs may be. Scanning means looking at a wide variety of sources of information to pick up the "blips," the early warning signs of impending change. As with a radar scan, once these signs of change are detected the organization can narrow its surveillance range to the region around the area of change, switching to monitoring. If the event proves to be important, the organization can then switch to tracking what's being written about the particular customers or application. As shown in Figure 4-8, surveillance techniques are particularly good for current and identified potential customers. But, as can be seen, scanning can even be useful for unidentified potential customers.

For example, a company providing training in the use of personal computer programs would want to scan the want ads to determine

	Customer classification		
Technique	Current	Identified potential	Unidentified potential
Surveillance	X	X	
Trend analysis	X	X	
Expert source	X	X	X
Integrative	X	X	X

Figure 4-8. Applicability of different types of customer needs analysis techniques.

who is hiring people and what personal computer (PC) skills they require. Articles on growth or problems of companies provide insight into needs, and finding out what companies have recently purchased computers would be beneficial.

Direct surveillance techniques are most often used by consumer product or service businesses. Watching how people shop and make decisions, electronic means of counting visits to different types of displays, and devices to monitor television viewing habits are a few of the many direct surveillance techniques.

Surveillance techniques, especially the direct ones, are most useful for determining present needs of customers. The reason is obvious: it's hard to find a future customer. However, surveillance over time can establish a trend which can be used to forecast future customer needs.

Trend Analysis

This is a place where the driving forces can be used directly. Faith Popcorn (1991)[1] has had an extensive surveillance program in effect aimed mostly at the social forces affecting the consumer market. She has identified 10 trends which are important in American society today:

- *Cocooning:* The need to protect oneself from the harsh, unpredictable realities of the outside world.
- *Fantasy adventure:* Modern age whets our desire for roads untaken.
- *Small indulgences:* Stressed-out consumers want to indulge in affordable luxury and seek ways to reward themselves.
- *Egonomics:* The sterile computer era breeds the desire to make a personal statement.
- *Cashing out:* Working women and men, questioning personal career satisfaction and goals, opt for simpler living.
- *Down-aging:* Nostalgic for their carefree childhood, baby boomers find comfort in familiar pursuits and products of their youth.
- *Staying alive:* Awareness that good health extends longevity leads to a new way of life.
- *The vigilante consumer:* The consumer manipulates marketing and the marketplace through pressure, protest, and politics.
- *99 lives:* Too fast a pace, too little time, cause societal schizophrenia and force us to assume multiple roles and adapt easily.

- *Save our society:* The country rediscovers a social conscience of ethics, passion, and compassion.

Popcorn demonstrates in her book the power to judge whether markets, products, and services are in tune with these trends. She states that in general practice it is important to have at least four of these trends supportive of a product or service.

Using the market-driven innovation methodology, the impacts of social trends such as those identified by Popcorn can be converted into potential customer needs, and customer need trends can be established. However, even in consumer markets, the other driving forces must be considered. For it is at the intersection of several driving forces and customer needs that significant opportunities exist.

Traditional methods of trend analysis involve the collection of historical data on customer needs for specific functions. Speed, accuracy, precision, performance, and defect levels are all examples of customer needs on which data can be accumulated over time. Once a trend line has been established by looking at the past, a forecast of the future can be made. A great deal of caution must be exercised at this point. Forecasting the future by looking at the past is a lot like trying to drive a car by looking at where you've been. It'll work fine as long as the road is straight (i.e., the future is like the past), there are no other cars on the road (i.e., competition does nothing), and there are no animals or people who cross in front of the car (i.e., no driving forces for change).

When forecasting the future from the past, always look at all the driving forces and ask these questions: "How will this driving force impact this trend? Will it cause the rate of change in needs to accelerate? To decelerate? Or will it create entirely new needs?"

Another method of forecasting needs is by looking at early adoptors. There is a generally accepted pattern of adoption of new products or ideas. *Early adoptors* are individuals or organizations who have advanced needs or who see the potential in new concepts long before the majority of the market. These early adoptors can act as precursors to the rest of the population if the lead-lag relationship has been established for previous products or services, or if it can be inferred from the behavior of the other markets. Determination of the characteristics of early adoptors is a well-refined science and art.

Expert Opinion

Expert opinion techniques constitute the bulk of customer research tools. Experts can, and in many cases must, be drawn from several categories:

- Customers

  Current
  Identified potential
  Unidentified potential

- Competitors

  Direct
  Indirect
  Structural

- Strategic relationships of the customers

  Customers of the customers
  Suppliers
  Others

- Researchers

  Academics
  Consultants
  Government personnel
  Association personnel
  Writers

- Opinion leaders

  Politicians
  Lobbyists
  Special interest groups
  Business leaders
  Government leaders

There are a wide variety of techniques to utilize the capabilities and knowledge of experts:

- Surveys

  Oral (personal, telephone)
  Written (paper, electronic)

- Group meetings (actual, nominal, electronic, or paper)

- Publications

The keys to effective utilization of experts are the proper choice of experts to represent the broad cross section of views required in order to get a good forecast of future needs; applying nonbiased methods of posing questions and analyzing answers, and applying methods to have the experts reflect on the impact of the driving forces on needs, are also essential.

Integrative

Integrative techniques can be as simple as having the experts reflect on the trend analysis, and, considering the driving forces, determine whether the trend will continue or not. They can employ complex and highly sophisticated computer models, built for the market being studied, that include the information developed through the other techniques. These models are built upon theory and experience of the way the facts being measured can together depict a future need.

It is imperative that information be obtained from a variety of different sources utilizing a variety of techniques. The results of all this research must then be analyzed and synthesized so that an adequate understanding of the customer's future needs can be established.

Importance of the Driving Forces

The driving forces for change are integrated in various ways into this process of customer needs forecasting. The driving forces are used to

- Determine what questions to ask and where to look for answers
- Sensitize minds to what to scan for
- Determine the impact on trends
- Select experts and guide their considerations
- Frame integrative models

Any one piece of information obtained about customers' future needs has a high probability of being wrong. Guiding the selection of what information to develop and how to interpret that information in light of the driving forces for change improves the probability that the new piece of information will be correct. Integrating several pieces of information from different sources and with different techniques guided by the driving forces for change reduces even further the probability of error.

Determining Customer Needs (Summary)

The following steps must be used to identify and classify customer needs:

1. Identify and list the types of customers in each of the three categories (current, identified potential, unidentified potential).

2. For each type of customer in each customer category, identify current needs, then consider the impact of the driving forces on those needs. For each type of customer, review all the driving forces for change. For each driving force, identify the new needs that will result for that type of customer.

3. For each need, determine the strength of the need. We have found that a qualitative scale is useful in some cases. We recommend that you use the following scale:

Symbol	Definition	Weight
O	No need	0
S	Small need	1
M	Medium need	2
L	Large need	3
XL	Extra large need	4

You may want to define this scale in terms of number of customers or priority to customers for your market if you wish to make the result more quantitative.

Technologies Impacting the Market

Technology is the practical application of knowledge. It manifests itself in a variety of forms:

- Methods
- Materials
- Systems

In a given market, the detailed examples of these can be classified into the three technology types—direct, supportive, and enabling. *Direct technologies* are those that are embedded in the product or service, and are visible to the customer. *Supportive technologies* are those involved in the research, development, design, manufacture, sale, and distribution of the product. *Enabling technologies* are those that allow improvements in the direct or supportive technologies.

Within a market, technologies exist at many levels. The choice of level of technology is the first key decision that an organization must

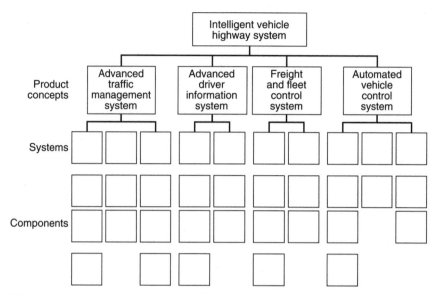

Figure 4-9. Technology structure for intelligent vehicle highway systems (IVHS).

make. For example, in the intelligent vehicle highway systems (IVHS) market, there is a complicated hierarchy of technologies (Figure 4-9). IVHS is an emerging market that consists of "smart" cars, "smart" highways, and the communication systems that link them. Technological change could be forecasted from the top level of IVHS all the way down to the metallurgy of integrated circuits, and at all the levels in between. A balance must be established between the amount of knowledge required to make a better decision and knowledge of how all the component technologies are going to behave.

The set point for the level of technologies to be forecasted is established through consideration of external and internal factors. The process of setting the level is holistic. A number of different questions must be answered. External questions to be answered are:

- What is the time frame?
- What is the market?
- Who is the customer?
- How are the needs articulated?
- What technologies are controlling the development of the market?
- How pervasive are the technologies?

With this set of questions, the organization is attempting to establish the level of technology that is controlling the development of the market. The organization must establish the level of technology that is key to fulfilling the needs of customers.

The second set of questions are related to the practicality of performing the forecast:

- What information is available?
- How much time is available to conduct the forecast?
- How much money is available?
- How many people are available?
- What are their capabilities?
- How dedicated are the people to the task?

The process shown in Figure 4-10 was developed for use in determining the key technologies of the IVHS market. After an extensive assessment by secondary research, a group of nine people with diverse

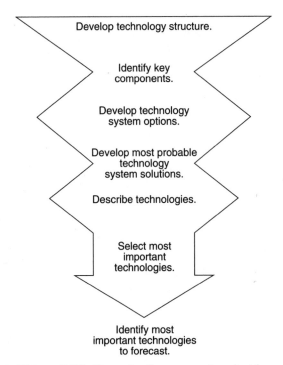

Figure 4-10. Example of a process to select key technologies.

backgrounds and responsibilities were brought together for a two-day workshop. At the conclusion of the workshop the level of technology had been set for the forecasts, and a small, manageable number of key technologies selected.

Assessing Technological Capability

The purpose of technology forecasting in this context is to assess the capability of the technology to meet the current and forecasted future needs of the customers. This requires in all cases the translation of customer needs, quite often expressed in terms of benefits, to specifications for price, function, and form, often thought of as attributes, both at the product level. These in turn must be converted into performance criteria for the technology. For example, throughput of traffic over a city's road system may ultimately depend upon the processing speed of microprocessors in remote locations. If this is a factor controlling the development of that part of IVHS, then the speed of microprocessors must be forecasted.

In making the assessment of future technological capabilities, there are three questions to be answered. Will the forecasted technological capability

- Be sufficient to meet customer needs?
- Be insufficient to meet customer needs?
- Surpass forecasted customer needs?

If the technological capability will satisfy customer needs, no further analysis is required. If it appears that technological capability will fall short of satisfying customer needs, the organization must decide if this is a limitation of the technology or the result of the amount of effort being given to advancing the state of the art. If it is a result of the amount of effort, what effort could the organization put in place that would advance the technology faster than the general market, thereby giving the organization a significant edge? If the capability of technology appears to be in excess of what is required by its application, then the question the organization must answer is, "What new needs is the availability of this technology likely to create?"

The organization may also want to assess its own technological capability versus that of the industry. The technology forecasting techniques facilitate this type of assessment.

Forecasting Technological Capability

The necessity to forecast technological capability derives from the requirement to fulfill the future needs of the customer. Once customer needs are understood, a logical next step is to discern which of the technologies available are likely to have capabilities to meet the needs at the specified future time in question. Forecasting is, however, more than trying to precisely pinpoint a single parameter. Our colleague, Ralph C. Lenz, whom many consider to be the father of technological forecasting, is fond of quipping, "It's better to be approximately right than precisely wrong!"[2] Joseph F. Coates eloquently states, "The burden of the work and the key to making forecasts credible has increasingly been assumed by the communications process rather than by the more abstract qualities of technical analysis."[3]

For today's environment, technology forecasting should be defined as the process of discovering and communicating probable technical capabilities in order to make better decisions and prevent surprises. Forget the academic exercises and concentrate on discovering the direction, rate, and nature of the changes taking place in the technologies in question. The tools available for accomplishing these tasks fall into four general categories of techniques: surveillance, trend analysis, expert opinion, and integrative. These are the same categories described above in our discussion of customer needs analysis. Now, their application is focused instead on the issues of technological capability. The techniques within the four are aimed at discerning the probable capabilities at the three levels of technology (direct, supportive, and enabling). The types of techniques used and the efforts employed to forecast are dependent on a series of both internal and external factors as previously discussed (see under "Technologies Impacting the Market"). The main reasons for conducting the forecast are to make better decisions, and to prevent surprises.

For forecasting purposes the surveillance category is made up of three technique (process) areas: scanning, monitoring, and tracking. *Scanning* is the process of looking broadly for events and trends that may imply an impact (threat or opportunity) upon the technical arena of particular interest. The activity is not unfocused, nor is it undirected; rather it is purposeful in effort to skim and detect. An individual who can discipline himself or herself to follow a scanning process can review great volumes of material in very short periods of time. Once potential information or data is detected, monitoring is used.

Monitoring is the process of specifically, and with a defined purpose, following the technological developments in a particular area.

Monitoring may be done by an individual or as a team or group effort. Not only are information and data gathered, they are analyzed for meaning and impact and the results communicated in some meaningful way. It is virtually impossible to develop a forecast without using monitoring techniques.

Tracking is the process of carefully and purposefully following a greatly narrowed range of technological development. The frequency of activity is greatly increased in a technological tracking mode. The results of this activity are of immediate value and can be used for both operational and strategic decisions.

Trend analysis as a category consists of many, mostly quantitative, techniques. We identify six techniques that have proven to be the more useful overall in business environments. They are precursor developments, trend extrapolation, the Pearl curve, the learning curve, substitution, and multiple substitution.

Forecasting using *precursor developments* can be done when a lead-lag relationship can be established between two technical areas. This is usually done by observation over a period of years, and establishing causal connections between the technical areas.

Trend extrapolation involves plotting key parameters of technical progress against time. From the results, regular development patterns can be discerned. An initial assumption can be made that the patterns, which are rooted in past developments, can be extended into the future for some period of time. In a large number of technical areas, it has been found that if progress is plotted versus time, the trace is linear on a semilog graph. This would represent a constant percentage rate of change.

The *Pearl curve*—named for the American demographer Raymond Pearl, who used it in demographic forecasting—is one example from a family of growth models. These techniques are often used to describe technological change patterns that resemble organic growth. The slope of the Pearl curve is a function of both the distance to go to the upper limit for growth and the distance already covered.

The *learning curve* is a production-driven performance technique. Its basic premise is that as the number of units produced doubles, the labor-hours per unit decrease by a constant factor.

Substitution analysis is used to forecast the rate at which one technology will replace another. The traditional approach involves the application of the Fisher-Pry model (J. C. Fisher and R. H. Pry 1971).[4] This model predicts characteristics loosely analogous to those of biological system growth. Many examples now exist for technology substitution.

Multiple substitution represents an increasingly common situation in which either more than one new technology is substituted for an old one or a single new technology is actually replacing more than one old technology.

The *expert opinion* forecasting category can be divided into three technique areas: interviews, surveys, and groups. In today's needs-driven environment the use of expert opinion for forecasting is imperative.

Interviews can be conducted under two basic conditions—structured and unstructured. Each type has advantages and disadvantages associated with it. However, given the value of people's time, structured interviews are optimal.

Surveys are conducted under many different formats and for many different reasons. They can vary from public opinion surveys administered by organizations such as Gallup to market research surveys done by the likes of *Good Housekeeping, Gentlemen's Quarterly, Working Woman,* or *Money* magazines. In large part what differs in a survey focused on technology development rather than market research or public opinion is the types of questions asked and who is included in the survey universe. One particular type of survey, the Delphi, can be adapted very well to the rigors of obtaining both quantitative and qualitative data.

There are also a myriad of *group* techniques which can be directed to gaining technological information for forecasting purposes. These group techniques may range from the familiar focus group to the highly structured and inclusive morphological analysis.

The *integrative* category of forecasting techniques consists of four technique areas: opportunity analysis, scenarios, cross-impact analysis, and mathematical models.

Opportunity analysis is the subject of this entire chapter.

Scenarios generally present in a narrative form the descriptions of multiple forecasts. They can provide a common context and a vehicle for presentation of very complex concepts and information.

Cross-impact approaches are designed to capture interactions between events or trends and to represent them formally in a cross-interaction model. Mathematical complexities, such as probabilities, can be deftly handled in a cross-impact matrix. With the advent of PCs and spreadsheet software the need to construct expensive models has diminished significantly.

A *mathematical model* uses equations to represent the system in which events occur. It requires significant time and effort to initiate and construct, and maintaining the model with current data is a necessary, yet onerous, task. The value of large mathematical models solely for technological forecasting is negligible in the current environment.

All these categories are useful and important to forecasting technological change. The forecaster must continuously update any and all projections as well as assess the impacts that the driving forces for change will have on the development rate and direction of technology.

Determining Technological Capability (Summary)

The following steps must be followed to determine the technological capability to meet the needs identified earlier:

1. Define the three types of technology (direct, supportive, and enabling) for this market.

2. Determine a comprehensive set of examples of each of the three types of technologies. From this list, identify the few key technologies that control the development of the products and systems to meet customer needs.

3. For each of the key technologies identified in each of the three types of technology, determine its current and future capability to meet the needs of the three categories of customers. This step can be as quantitative as you want it to be. Technology-forecasting techniques are often essential in the determination of technological capability over the time frame of the analysis. Match the technology-forecasting technique to the application.

4. For each technology, determine the strength of the technological capability against the needs of the market. We have found it useful to convert the quantitative capability forecast to a qualitative statement using the following scale:

Symbol	Definition	Weight
O	No capability to meet need	0
S	Some capability to meet need	1
M	Meets needs	2
L	Exceeds needs	3
XL	Greatly exceeds needs	4

What Is the Competition?

Customers provide the "pull" in the market. Their needs attract competition, vying to provide solutions to those needs. Technology developed by the set of competitors satisfies those needs but also can create new needs through advanced capability. Technology therefore can be the "push" of the market. Competition is the "clash" in the market as competitors each seek superior positions.

There are three different types of competition:

- Direct
- Indirect
- Structural

Direct competitors attempt to satisfy the same need in the same manner. *Indirect competitors* attempt to satisfy the same need but in different ways. *Structural competitors* attempt to do away with the need.

For example, consider the airline industry. The airline companies are moving goods and people from place to place. American Airlines, Delta, and Continental are all direct competitors. Indirect competitors are numerous. Examples of indirect competition are bus companies, trains, ships, and cars. A structural competitor to the airline industry is telecommunications and computers. Video conferences, faxes, phones, and electronic mail are attempting to do away with the need for face-to-face meetings. In one profoundly large blunder, an airline company held a national meeting of its management team to address its strategic plan for its future via teleconferencing to save time and money.

Organizations often have considerable knowledge of their direct competitors. But in many cases, even with a lot of information on direct competitors, they lack the understanding of the competitor's strategy which is key to understanding that competitor's response to future needs. Rarely do organizations study and understand their indirect competitors, and almost never do they consider structural competition. This is a significant failing, for there is considerable wisdom to be gained by examining these two areas of competition.

IBM's failure to understand the power of semiconductor integrated circuitry to produce microprocessors and the impact they would have on computer systems is a significant contemporary example. IBM did not understand the indirect competition of PCs and workstations with its central processor strategy. The Pullman Company, which produced and staffed quality sleeping accommodations on passenger trains, did not understand the structural competition of air travel. And RCA, one of the early developers of transistor technology, failed to comprehend their impact on vacuum tubes, and therefore the power of indirect competitors like Texas Instruments.

The pharmaceutical companies that commercialized the polio vaccines were structural competitors of iron lung manufacturers. In the 1930s, the manufacturers of cooked canned foods were structural competitors of the ice delivery services for iceboxes. Later, the mechanical refrigerator companies were indirect competitors of icebox companies. Currently, the marketers of irradiated and aseptically packaged uncooked foods are structural competitors for the makers of refrigerators.

Dick Davis, a futurist for Whirlpool who foresaw the impact of wrinkle-free fabrics, a structural competitor to irons, and who helped Whirlpool capitalize on that change said, "No company ever gets struck by the future in the forehead. They get it in the temple!"[5] Organizations do a reasonable, although sometimes myopic, job of understanding their direct competition, but they frequently fall short of identifying, understanding, and integrating into the organization the impacts of indirect and structural competitors.

Competitive Response

The process of understanding the competitive response to the strategic needs discovered earlier in this chapter begins with the definition of the three categories of competitors. Then specific competitors are listed and ranked in order of current importance to the organization. Sometimes it is not possible, or practical, to list specific indirect or structural competitors. In this case, identify classes of these types of competitors and describe them.

The next steps involve the development of an understanding of the competitor's current strategy. This is followed by an assessment of each competitor's response to the forecasted needs. The techniques for understanding competitors' strategies and their likely response to future needs can be categorized in the same way as needs forecasting and technology-forecasting techniques: surveillance, trend analysis, expert opinion, and integrative techniques.

This is not a book on competitive analysis. Our purpose here is to give an overview of the techniques, and, more important, show how to integrate them into an overall opportunity and threat analysis.

Many of the technology-forecasting techniques can be and are applied to competitive analysis. It's just that their focus is shifted from the technology to the competitors. Some of the customer needs analysis and forecasting techniques are also applicable here. Three of the techniques unique to competitive analysis are

- Benchmarking

- Reverse engineering
- Executive analysis

Benchmarking has been made very popular because of the stress on quality and the focus on "best" practices. *Benchmarking* is a way to obtain and share information about processes used within organizations. *Reverse engineering,* buying a competitor's product and analyzing its components and its design, and inferring processes can give concise, direct information about a competitor's current capability. *An analysis of executives' personalities* can add information on the competitor's likely response to change.

Assessing Competitive Response (Summary)

The following steps must be used to identify the competitive response to the needs identified in the previous section:

1. Define the types of competition (direct, indirect, and structural) for this market.

2. Identify the types of competition and list as many specific examples as reasonable in each of the three categories.

3. For each competitor type identified, determine the competitive response to the needs. It is helpful here to reconsider all the needs each time an innovation response is determined.

4. For each response determined, identify the strength of the response. Use the same five-point scale as was used in the determination of customer needs.

Additional Insights on Technology

At this point it is useful to revisit the assessment of technology. Often, the direct technologies considered are all those used by the direct competitors. Add to the technology list those that are associated with the indirect and structural competitors. Select those that are key to development of your organization's competitors' ability to meet the needs of customers. Use technology-forecasting techniques to ascertain if the organization's indirect competitors are going to be able to replace the organization's products or whether the organization's structural competitors are going to be able to do away with the need for those products.

Synthesizing Market Opportunity or Threat

The synthesizing of customer needs, technological capability, and competitive response into a view of the opportunity and threat in a market provides significant insight. However, the organization should not lose sight of the details of the analysis of or the insights that have been developed by the process it has gone through to get to this point. It is useful throughout this synthesis process to keep a "trail" from the synthesized statement to the details that made it up. For while the synthesis is helpful in creating a strategy and comparing the opportunity and threat to the organizational culture, it is from the details that project focus is determined.

The process of synthesis begins with the definition of the types of innovation appropriate for this market. This means taking the definitions of the class (incremental, distinctive, and breakthrough) and nature (product, process, and procedure) of innovation (see Chapter 2) and applying them to the organization's market. Remembering the fourth principle of being market driven, it is useful to define innovation in terms of the organization's current customers in the current time frame.

The forecasted needs of the customers then become the key to structuring an innovation map. Each of the needs is classified by nature and class, and a weighted aggregate innovation map of the needs created (Figure 4-11). The same method is used for technological capability and competitive response. It is ideal, although not necessary, to track each individual need through this synthesis. For each forecasted need, what is the anticipated technological capability and the probable competitive response? Needs for which there is little or no competitive response but for which there is anticipated technological capability can be opportunities for the organization. Strong needs for which there is significant competitive response can be threats to the organization.

The three innovation maps are then combined into one map that represents a summary of the innovation opportunity and threat within the market. There is no absolute algebra to create the summary innovation map. Common sense and intuition must prevail. However, the authors have found the following method useful.

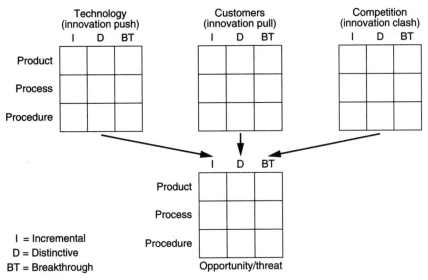

Figure 4-11. Innovation map of market opportunity.

Creating the Summary Innovation Map

To determine the innovation opportunity in the market, consider each cell of the innovation maps for customers, competition, and technology separately. Start with the customer innovation map. Compare it to the technology innovation map. If the capability is there, leave the result at the strength of customer need. If the technological capability is not there, reduce the result from the strength of the need. If there is more technological capability than needed, consider increasing the result from the strength of the needs. Use extreme caution here. Just because technological capability exists does not mean that there will be customer need. Before increasing the resultant from the customer need, go all the way back to the individual needs, types of customers, and driving forces. Make an assessment of whether the customer need will be increased by the existence of the technological capability, or if new needs will be created.

Now, look at the competitive response for the type of innovation the organization is considering. Figure 4-12 shows some guidelines for synthesizing the three innovation maps into an opportunity map. Please remember that these are only guidelines. Use your own judgment, and continually refer to the sources of the average results. This is where the real wisdom and power of the technique lies.

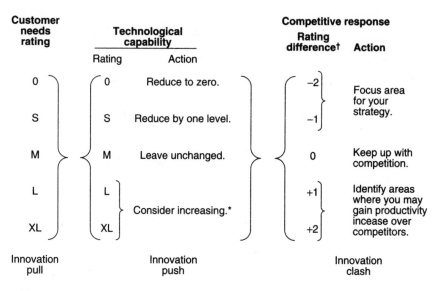

*Review details of needs and capability

†Difference between customer needs rating (average strength of need) and competitive response rating.

Figure 4-12. Guideline for synthesizing opportunity innovation map.

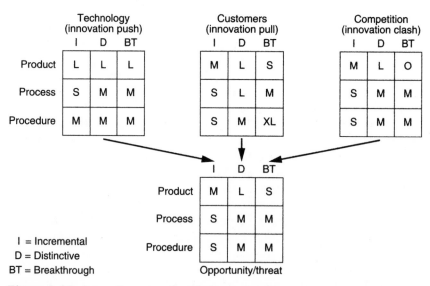

Figure 4-13. Innovation map of market opportunity.

Enter the results into an opportunity innovation map as shown in Figure 4-13. The opportunity analysis is now completed. The organization's opportunity innovation map now shows the types of innovation that will meet future customer needs for the time frame chosen, and which types of innovation will provide potential competitive advantage.

For those needs for which there wasn't enough technological capability forecasted, review the needs and technology forecasts. Can the organization advance the technology ahead of the industry to take advantage of the needs? Make this assessment, and utilize this information later when constructing the organization's strategy.

In the example of an opportunity innovation map shown in Figure 4-13, an opportunity exists for breakthrough products because, even though the needs of customers are small, there is plenty of technological capability and no competitive activity. There is also the potential for the organization to significantly advance the capability of the technology for breakthrough procedures. There is a significant demand for this type of innovation and only modest competitive response which is in line with the forecasted technological capability. If the organization can advance the technology sufficiently, it can gain a competitive advantage here.

References

1. Faith Popcorn, *The Popcorn Report*, Harper Business, New York, 1992.
2. Ralph C. Lenz, Technology Futures, Inc., Private Communication.
3. Alan L. Porter, A. Thomas Roper, Thomas W. Mason, Frederick A. Rossini, and Jerry Banks, *Forecasting and Management of Technology*, Wiley, New York, 1991.
4. J. C. Fisher and R. H. Pry, "A Simple Substitutional Model of Technological Change," *Technology Forecasting and Social Change*, Vol. 3, 1971, pp. 75–88.
5. Richard Davis, Technology Futures, Inc., Private Communication.

5

Developing a Strategy to Take Advantage of the Opportunity

Strategic Thinking

An organization's strategy should flow from the analysis of the market opportunity and threats, aspirations of its people, and the needs of its stakeholders (Figure 5-1). Strategy development encompasses the creation of a vision, selection of a mission, setting of goals, and development of a strategic plan.

A *strategic plan* is the organization's interpretation of the market opportunity. It is its way to capitalize on the market opportunity based on its

- Vision
- Mission
- Goals
- Capabilities

A strategic plan is organization dependent because no two organizations have the same vision, mission, goals, and capabilities. Therefore, even if two organizations uncover the same opportunity, they are likely to perceive it differently. A strategic plan is a way to minimize or

Figure 5-1. Strategic thinking.

avoid threats. It is a method to effectively utilize the organization, to satisfy the organization's stakeholders, and a way to provide competitive differentiation.

To develop a strategic plan, the organization must:

- Understand the market in which it operates
- Understand the needs and aspirations of people in the organization
- Synthesize the needs of market, stakeholders, and people into a vision
- Establish a shared vision
- Select a mission, set goals, and develop the plan together with the organization
- Create the strategic plan to capitalize on the opportunity, avoid or minimize the threats, and meet business needs as stated in the vision, mission, and goals

The hierarchy of elements in the strategy is shown in Figure 5-2. The vision must be created first, followed by the mission, goals, and strategic plan.

Innovation Strategy

An innovation strategy is only good for a finite amount of time. One of the worst mistakes an organization can make is to assume that because an innovation strategy was successful it will always be successful. The environment shifts, customers' needs change, competition gets smart, technologies improve, and the organization itself evolves.

The market-driven innovation methodology's perspective on strategy differs from others in that an innovation change can have a complex pattern as represented by the innovation map. Our innovative strategies are more complex than just being a "low-cost leader "or

- Vision ⟶ Purpose

- Mission ⟶ Areas of business operation

- Goals ⟶ Objectives to be reached

- Strategic plan ⟶ Way to accomplish objectives

Figure 5-2. Strategy development.

"niche creator," for example. There are nine different types of innovation and therefore at least nine different principal foci of strategic intent, and there are even more complex secondary and tertiary patterns. The innovation map is a powerful tool for creating and depicting innovation strategies.

Once an innovation strategy has been selected, there is the establishment of an immediate vulnerability. On the competitive battlefield, an innovation strategy is like a decision to attack. Each movement creates the opportunity for a response. Each innovation strategy has included within it the seeds of its own destruction. This implies that strategies should be living concepts that link markets, organizational capabilities, business objectives, and individual needs.

A Classic Example: The U.S. Automobile Industry

A classic example illustrating these observations about innovation strategies is the U.S. automobile industry. There were five major stages in the development of strategy in the auto industry from the 1820s until the 1970s, which we will discuss in the following sections.

Experimenters and Hobbyists: The Early Days

The search for a self-propelled wheeled vehicle began with Cugnot's steam-powered tricycle. Other technological competitors followed, with internal combustion engines and electric motors providing energy sources. During this period the fastest car was, surprisingly, an electric vehicle.

From the 1880s to the 1920s there was a rapid proliferation of different versions of the automobile. Hundreds of companies were created, each with its unique approach. Carriage shops in many cases acted as the incubator. To own a car during this period required daring and at least a modicum of mechanical ability. Purchasers were the early adopters, experimenters, and hobbyists, who weren't concerned about repairing the frequent breakdowns, and certainly not totally dependent on the auto as a means of transportation or business. There were few roads, and those were of poor quality.

The breakthrough innovation of Cugnot resulted in many distinctive and incremental product innovations. Competitors were searching for the right technologies and the right configurations to meet market needs. The thrust of this innovation activity is shown in Figure 5-3 as an arrow from the "breakthrough product" section of the figure. There was not a lot of focus on process or procedure innovations.

Search and Learn: The Development of the Ford Model T

When Henry Ford began his search for the perfect car, there was still a great deal of technological uncertainty. No one knew for sure which engine type would win. Certainly no one knew which configuration would best fit the market. Ford went through a process of searching, trying different configurations of internal combustion engine autos, to find the car for the "common man." The "Model T" designation was not

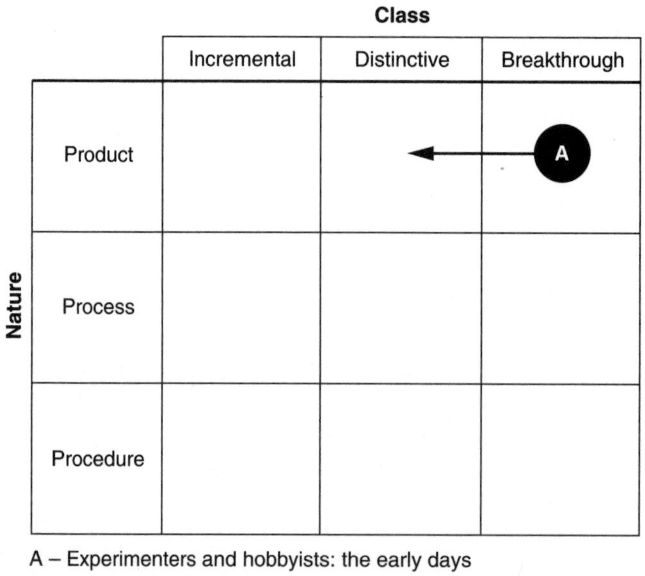

A – Experimenters and hobbyists: the early days

Figure 5-3. The U.S. automobile industry: Experimenters and hobbyists—the early days.

capricious but the result of trials A through S, which culminated in 1908 in the Model T. The major innovation strategy during this period was a continuation of the distinctive product innovations of the past, along with a movement toward incremental product innovations (Figure 5-4).

A Car for Everyone: Exploiting the Model T

Ford correctly recognized that the driving forces for change in the United States were creating a need for cheap, reliable, independent methods of transportation. He correctly understood that if he could rationalize the manufacturing system and drive the cost down, he could capture a large share of the market. To improve the reliability and decrease the cost, Ford instituted a series of product, process, and procedure innovations:

- Product innovations

    Four-cylinder engine (cost, efficiency)
    Works completely enclosed (more reliable)
    Durable (stood up to bumps)
    Reliable (didn't strip gears)
    $825 price (competitors', $2000)

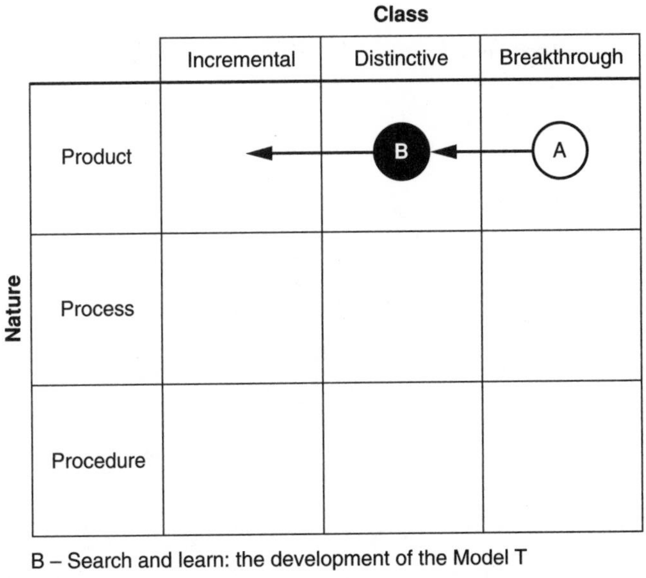

B – Search and learn: the development of the Model T

Figure 5-4. The U.S. automobile industry: Search and learn—the development of the Model T.

- Process innovations

    Reinforced-concrete factory with windows/skylights
    Interchangeability of parts
    Moving assembly line
    Task/part segmentation

- Procedure innovations

    High pay (double competitors)
    Nonstop eight-hour shift rotations

The results of all of these innovations plus an incredible number of subsequent incremental innovations produced impressive cost reductions (Figure 5-5).

An example that has been reported shows the depth of the rationalization. Ford requested that gears be shipped in wooden boxes, and he specified the dimensions of the pieces of wood in the boxes. This wood was just the right size to be used as is for the floorboards of the cars. Ford had all the cars painted black, and all the parts black. This maximized the interchangeability of the parts, simplifying inventory. The joke was that you could get any color Model T you wanted as long as it was black.

The results were impressive. Ford created the auto industry and dominated it for years. Some people even credit him with the creation of the consumer society we live in. He made the cars cheap enough to be purchased and paid the workers well enough that they could become consumers.

This innovation strategy is depicted in Figure 5-6. Ford took the

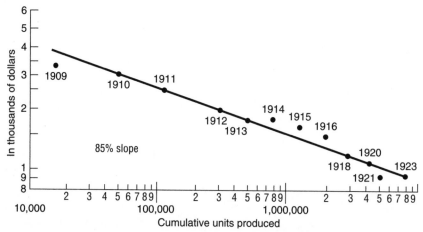

Figure 5-5. Price of the Model T, 1909–1923 (average list price in 1958 dollars).

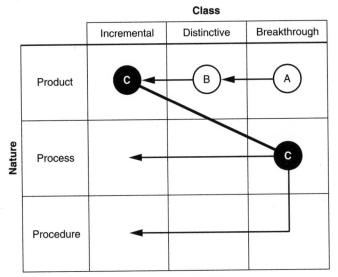

C – Car for everyone: exploiting the Model T

Figure 5-6. The U.S. automobile industry: A car for everyone—exploiting the Model T.

results of what he had learned about the product design and configuration and focused on breakthrough, distinctive, and incremental process and procedure innovations.

Spectacularly successful as this strategy was, Ford made the mistake of believing in it too much. On his deathbed, he is reported to have said that the only thing wrong with the Model T was that it stopped selling. As Abernathy and Wayne (1982)[1] have pointed out:

> The strategy of cost minimization singlemindedly followed with the Model T was a spectacular success. But the changes that accompanied it carried the seeds of trouble that affected the organization's ability to vary its product, alter its cost structure, and continue to innovate.

From Rural Utility Vehicle to Living Room on Wheels: GM's Response

Environmental forces were at work in this market to create change. People's social values were changing. They wanted more choice, more comfort, more luxury. Women were becoming drivers, and the open carriages and hand-crank starter were definite drawbacks. People began to have more disposable income and attached status to the type of automobile they owned. Porter (1985)[2] explains that

> The classic example of the risks of cost leadership is the Ford Motor Company of the 1920s. Ford had achieved unchallenged cost leadership through limitation of models and varieties, aggressive backward integration, highly-automated facilities, and aggressive pursuit of lower costs through learning. Learning was facilitated by the lack of model changes. Yet as incomes rose and many buyers had already purchased a car and were considering their second, the market began to place more of a premium on styling, model changes, comfort, and closed rather than open cars. Customers were willing to pay a price premium to get such features. General Motors stood ready to capitalize on this development with a full line of models. Ford faced enormous costs of strategic readjustment given the rigidities created by heavy investments in cost minimization of an obsolete model.

GM took advantage of Ford's preoccupation with an obsolete strategy and developed cars for everyone. They offered different price ranges, flexibility of choice, optional features, and a host of technological innovations, not the least of which was Kettering's electric starter and battery system. Alfred Sloan, the founder of GM, was quoted by Abernathy and Wayne[3] as saying,

> Mr. Ford...had frozen his policy in the Model T,...preeminently an open-car design. With its light chassis, it was unsuited to the heavier closed body, and so in less than two years [by 1923], the closed body made the already obsolescing design of the Model T noncompetitive as an engineering design....
>
> The old [GM] strategic plan of 1921 was vindicated to a "T," so to speak, but in a surprising way as to the particulars. The old master had failed to master change....His precious volume, which was the foundation of his position, was fast disappearing. He could not continue losing sales and maintain his profits. And so, for engineering and marketing reasons, the Model T fell....In May 1927....he shut down his great River Rouge plant completely and kept it shut down for nearly a year to retool, leaving the field to Chevrolet unopposed and opening it up for Mr. Chrysler's Plymouth. Mr. Ford regained sales leadership again in 1929, 1930, and 1935, but, speaking in terms of generalities, he had lost the lead to General Motors.

GM's innovation strategy is depicted in Figure 5-7. While GM certainly produced many process and procedure innovations, the principal innovation strategy was a return to a distinctive and incremental product innovation thrust. As a result of correctly reading the driving

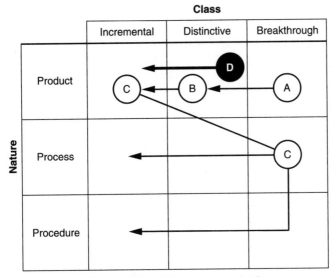

D – From rural utility vehicle to living room on wheels

Figure 5-7. The U.S. automobile industry: From rural utility vehicle to living room on wheels.

forces for change and interpreting their impact on consumers, GM dominated the auto market for a number of years. However, as Abernathy, Clark, and Kantrow (1983)[4] point out, even when imports began to make inroads,

> [t]he comfortable maturity into which American automobile makers drifted during the 1950s and 1960s kept all such potentially disquieting questions at bay. Like their counterparts in other manufacturing industries, executives in Detroit felt they had found the key to unlock forever the boundaries of a secure domestic market. Their confidence was soon to cost them dearly.

Synthesizing Market Demands: Development of Toyota

In the 1950s and 1960s there were new driving forces for change. The United States was being suburbanized. People were fleeing from the inner cities and were in the process of creating the present-day megalopolises of Los Angeles, Houston, and Atlanta, to name just a few. The car became essential to get around cities that were created by and for the car. But even more than that, the people left in the suburbs needed a second car. People had enough disposable income for two cars but would have liked to have a smaller, cheaper car for the second car.

There was a niche entry at the low end, Volkswagen, and the German manufacturer found a very successful niche market. Detroit tried to respond by building small cars, but found that it could not produce small cars cheaply enough to compete. The only way that Detroit could take cost out was to reduce quality, and that produced some disastrous results and eventual return to the big-car formula. To quote Abernathy, Clark, and Kantrow:[5]

> In retrospect, then, we can see that Detroit's early flirtation with a new calculus of automobile design and production was at base a continuation of past practice, a somewhat half-hearted attempt to view the competitive dynamics of the industry in different terms. Just how strong a grip the logic of large car production had on the industry can be seen in the compacts' steady increase in size and weight during the years they were in production. Indeed, each year seemed to bring a few more inches and a few more pounds until, by the late 1960s, even a once trim car like the Falcon had added a foot in length and 500 pounds in weight. Detroit, in effect, first tried to build small cars by making little big cars.

Detroit's insistence on following its old business theory caused a backlash. There were attacks on the quality and safety of the small cars, and a general discrediting of the large U.S. automakers. Kotler et al. (1985)[6] describe the situation:

> The U.S. automobile companies ignored these warning signals and continued to build larger and more expensive regular automobiles. This total ignorance of consumer demand led to significant negative car buyer attitudes—a pro-foreign, anti-Detroit syndrome. As Donald Peterson, vice president of car planning and research for Ford's Product Development Group, observed: "People believed that we make too many changes for change's sake—i.e., non-functional changes. There's a credibility gap. People don't believe our advertising. It has done more harm than good."

Toyota was watching. They saw the success of Volkswagen, the driving forces for change, the changing needs of auto buyers, and the power of innovation to redefine the small auto with quality. As Kotler et al.[7] state,

> As strategic planners of the highest order, the Japanese aim their marketing efforts, not at where the competition is situated, but at where they think the competitive battlefield will be in the future.

Toyota did extensive market research in the United States using

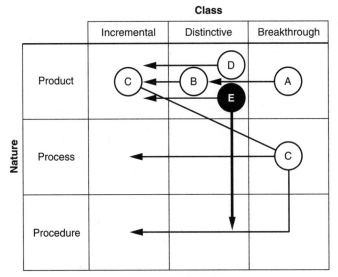

E – Synthesizing market demands: Japan's entry

Figure 5-8. The U.S. automobile industry: Synthesizing market demands—Japan's entry into the U.S. automobile market.

Volkswagen as the prototype. They used U.S. market research firms and U.S. data, and beat us at our own game. Their first entry, the Toyopet, was not a success, but they stuck with their new business theory and the result was a restructuring of the market.

The innovation strategy of Toyota is shown in Figure 5-8. They focused on distinctive product, process, and procedure innovations. Then their thrust was incremental innovations across the board. Eventually, Toyota became the market leader.

Types of Strategies

There are many different types of strategies. Strategies can be driven by

- Technology
- Customer
- Competition
- Stakeholders
- Strategic relationships
- Organizational capability

- Culture
- Personal vision

In some situations, each may be appropriate. In most situations, following just one to the exclusion of others will result in failure. However, in all cases, a market-driven strategy can be successful. In a market-driven strategy, all the different types of strategies are considered and the appropriate one for the situation selected.

Strategy Development Process

The process for market-driven strategy development is shown in Figure 5-9. Several terms are used in this figure. For an organization a *vision* provides purpose. A *mission* defines the area of business operation. *Goals* are objectives to be reached. The *strategic plan* details how to accomplish the goals, within the mission, to make the vision a reali-

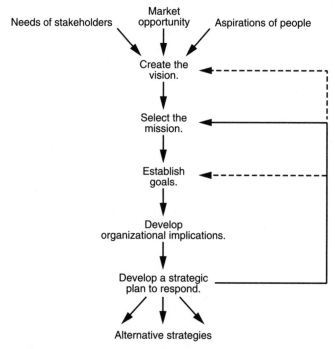

Figure 5-9. Strategy development.

ty. After the market opportunity has been defined, strategy development begins by creating the vision for the organization. This is followed by selection of a mission and establishment of goals. Once these are understood, the organizational implications can be developed. From all this information, strategies can be developed to take advantage of the opportunities, avoid or minimize the threats, and fully and effectively utilize the organization.

Organizational Change

A strategy is the road map for change. Because of the interaction of the driving forces for change with customer needs, technological capabilities, and competitive responses, the market the organization wishes to serve is constantly changing. In order for the organization to remain competitive in a global market, it must change to align its projects, resources, and culture to the redefined opportunity. The strategy is the link between the changing world outside the organization and the world inside the organization that needs to change.

The internal implications of the organization's strategy are enormous and must be addressed within the strategy. A strategy focused only on the outside world will not be effective or efficient. The organization's strategy calls for the organization, and thus the people in it, to change, and gives them the path. If the organization is motivated to change, change will result, and innovation will follow. If that innovation can be focused continually on the market, the organization will be successful.

For individuals to change, they must first have the desire to change. If an individual has the desire to change, he or she may develop the intention to change. If intention develops, the person may act on that intention.

The process of facilitating this series of events is motivation. Motivation is not a thing, it is a process. To motivate someone to change, a compelling reason for change must be developed and communicated to that person in a language the person understands. If this creates the desire to change, the intention to change may develop if the way to achieve change is developed and communicated. If the person believes that the way is credible, plausible, and likely to result in success, the person will develop the intention to change. If trust has been established between the person and the organization of which he or she is a member, the person will act on that intention and begin to change. At this stage, change is still delicate. If there are no positive results that are obvious to the individual, he or she may revert to old patterns of behavior, or even worse, hunker down and wait for the storm to blow over. This behavior is devastating to the organization. However, if positive results are obtained in the early stages, and the individual sees the long-term perspective, significant change can be effected.

The processes of change in an organization therefore become the "four E's" (Figure 5-10). If the organization ennobles, enables, empowers, and encourages, positive change will result. The result of the four E's is a fifth E, enjoyment. The people in the organization will enjoy what they are doing even if the change path is difficult.

Much has been written and said about *empowerment* in today's business world. Its virtues have become almost common wisdom, and it is offered as a panacea for almost all problems. But empowerment without ennoblement and enablement is a recipe for disaster. Just telling people that they are empowered to change without giving them the tools of change and the channel of change is sure to fail.

The ennobling process gives people the reason for change and thus justifies the extraordinary risk and hard work it takes to go through change. To *ennoble* someone is to give them a higher purpose and give meaning to their work. And as work is the main activity of most people's lives, if their work is ennobled, their life can become ennobled. In strategy development, ennoblement is provided by the vision.

Enabling means providing the tools for change, giving the people the weapons they need to fight the battles of change. Many of these extend beyond the scope of strategy development, but the two elements of strategy that do apply here are mission and goals. Missions and goals can be hierarchical, subdivided down so that every individual sees how their piece fits into the organization's strategy.

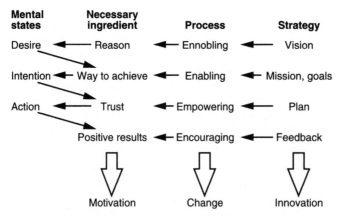

Figure 5-10. Organizational change processes.

The strategic plan empowers individuals to act. It tells them how to go about the process of change.

Encouragement is provided by feedback of the positive results. This is one of the reasons why a good measurement system must be established. Measurements can also be hierarchical, so that each individual can be measured on their contributions. Measurements can also be time phased. Some measurements can be developed that will show results earlier than those that reflect the significant organizational change.

Creating a Vision

Creating a vision (Figure 5-11) which can take advantage of the opportunity, meet the business objectives of the organization, and effectively energize the people who work in the organization is one of the most important and creative things that a manager can do. It can turn a manager into a leader.

Many organizational vision statements have no spirit. They are weak and platitudinous. This type of formulation must be avoided. The vision will not only not accomplish what you want it to but will be detrimental to the morale of the organization.

A vision

- Provides a bridge from the present to a future state
- Is a target that beckons
- Depicts a future state that does not exist and never existed before
- Confers status
- Bridges between the market, the business, and people

Figure 5-11. The vision connection.

- Energizes the organization

To create a vision, consider the following:

- Decide what will excite people.
- Focus the vision on strategic advantages.
- Think about how your organization adds value to others.
- Make the vision simple enough to be used to make decisions.
- Develop a strategy to gain a broad base of support for the vision.
- State it in the present tense.

Use both informal and formal channels of communication. Make sure that everyone shares in the vision including employees, customers, stakeholders, and suppliers. In the process of gaining support for the vision, the vision may need to be modified. Experience of many leaders has shown that it is wise to alter the vision to gain the maximum amount of support. It is important that the vision be communicated to and shared by the organization and its stakeholders.

The following are some characteristics of a good vision. It must

- Be short and succinct
- Be clear and unambiguous
- Have meaning to everyone in the organization
- Lead to distinctiveness
- Be innovation-rich
- Provide reason for extraordinary effort
- Be sustainable through mission, product, technology, and organizational changes
- Be identifiable with the greater good

A good vision will

- Help people feel significant
- Establish the value of learning and competence
- Unite people and give them a collective identity
- Make work exciting, not by pushing, but through identification with common goals
- Establish integrity, dedication, openness, creativity, and courage in the organization

- Encourage people to think longer term
- Allow people to understand the whole
- Encourage people to exert influence beyond their bounds
- Unite multiple, sometimes conflicting, constituencies
- Foster thinking in terms of renewal

In Chapter 4, identification of the opportunity in the marketplace was discussed. The business objectives should be known for your organization. The vision must link both of these to the various needs of the people in the organization. What do they want to accomplish with their lives? Why are they working for this organization? These are questions that must be answered if a good vision is to be established.

Many surveys have been conducted in all cultures of what people want to accomplish with their lives. This kind of cultural information is basic to an understanding of the specific characteristics and values of the people in the organization. For example, Figure 5-12 lists the top seven things Americans say they want out of their lives. To determine what the people in a particular organization want to accomplish with their lives, surveys, interviews, and focus groups can be designed and conducted. This, together with information for your culture similar to that in Figure 5-12, can be used to help formulate a vision.

Visioning does not lend itself to linear processes. It is basically intuitive, holistic, iterative, and synthetic. It is advisable to work with a group of people who represent a cross section of the organization in a focus group or nominal group setting. The vision statement, once created, must be "socialized" with ever larger groups of people, modifying it along the way, until the entire organization and its stakeholders have adopted it.

In summary, to establish a vision, the organization must know how to learn what its members believe is important, credible, and relevant. Then it must identify the directions the members find exciting, develop a positive vision to embody this, and communicate it to the people in language they understand.

Selecting a Mission

A *mission* defines the area of business chosen to help make the vision a reality. It puts boundaries around the organization to channel and focus its efforts. A well-selected mission makes the organization more effective in its operations. It defines the area of the opportunity that

1. People want more control over their own lives and over the destinies of their families.

2. People want opportunities to learn and develop throughout their lives.

3. People want interesting work/meaningful activity/important roles which offer recognition and rewards.

4. People want to participate in and actively experience life rather than watch or experience others performing.

5. People want challenges to their creative/problem-solving abilities.

6. People want to live and work among open, happy, trusting people.

7. People do not want to be unwillingly or unwittingly jeopardized.

Figure 5-12. What do Americans say they want out of life? (Summarized from over 100 attitude and opinion surveys.) (*source: David Pearce Snyder and Gregg Edwards*, Future Forces, *Foundation of the American Society of Associated Executives, 1984.*)

will be addressed. As a result, it selects the competition the organization will face. Since it narrows the organization's focus, it can lead to the development of sustainable competitive advantage.

Establishing Goals

Goals are measurable objectives that the organization must reach within an identified time frame. Often it is advisable to establish several different time frames for goals, for example, periods of five and ten years. Goals are steps on the organization's way to actualizing the vision within the chosen area of business. Goals must be attainable but outside the current reach of the organization. The organization must need to be innovative to reach the goals. If the goals are too easily attained, they will not serve to motivate the organization. If the goals are impossible to reach, frustration will develop, and morale will drop.

It is imperative to monitor progress on the path to realization of the goals. This means that the degree of attainment of the goals must be measurable; therefore, a measurement system must be established every time a goal is established.

Goals are indicators of what's worth achieving in and by the organization. They become the "glue" for the organizational structure. Goals can be segmented, and each piece related to the whole. This creates a hierarchy of purpose, and it gives people in the organization a way to identify with the vision. A vision can sometimes be too lofty; people can buy into the vision but not see how they can contribute. Hierarchical goals provide individuals with a way to help the organization and themselves realize the vision.

Developing Organizational Implications

The next step in the process is to develop the organizational implications, positive and negative, of the opportunity, vision, mission, and goals. This is best done by considering five areas of the business:

- Organizational structures
- Communication systems
- Incentives
- Education
- Management systems

The organizational structure area includes, for example,

- Mission structures
- Programs for support of concepts generated by the organization, such as creative development proposals, invention support, and an innovation review board
- Programs to facilitate the development of intraorganizational experience, such as internal consulting, task forces, study groups, quality circles, and temporary assignments
- Programs and structures to promote learning or developmental assignments, such as fellowships and sabbaticals
- Programs and structures to encourage mentoring

Examples of communication systems are

- Internal and external publications
- Databases and computer conferences
- Internal and external professional societies

- Libraries
- Seminars and symposia
- Programs to promote informal communication both inside and outside the organization

Incentives cover things such as

- "Multiple-path" career paths. ("Dual-ladder" and "triple-ladder" promotional programs have been used to increase the development of managers, technical professionals, and in the triple-ladder case, entrepreneurs.)
- Award programs for suggestions, innovations, inventions, and progress
- Salary programs to promote continued development
- Recognition programs
- Intangibles such as

  Valuing "creative" failure higher than "safe" path
  Access to power tools of change
  Time to pursue innovative projects
  Ability to be involved in more innovative programs
  Dress codes
  Out-of-company activities
  Work atmosphere

Education program examples are programs for

- Personal skills development
- Technical skills development
- Management skills development
- Development of integrative skills such as creativity, innovation, professionalism, forecasting, and leadership

Management systems must accomplish the following:

- Establish the shared vision of innovation.
- Set strategic direction.
- Provide innovation objectives.
- Create innovation enhancement programs, guidelines, reviews, and measurements.
- Assure commitment.

- Demonstrate patience.
- Be flexible.

The organizational implications are developed by going through each statement or fact in the opportunity, vision, mission, and goals carefully and developing a list of implications of each statement for each of the five categories listed at the beginning of this section. When a list of implications has been created, assess the importance of each. They will be used to help develop the strategic plan.

Developing a Strategic Plan

The strategic plan must inform the organization about how to accomplish the goals within the mission in order to reach the vision. A strategic plan must embody

- Decisions that must be made today but which affect the future
- Major questions of resource allocation that determine the organization's long-term results
- The calculated means by which the organization will deploy its resources to accomplish its purpose under the most advantageous circumstances.
- The methods to establish a competitive edge, allowing the organization to serve its customers better than its competitors
- The broad principles by which a company hopes to secure an advantage over competitors, an attractiveness to buyers, and a full utilization and activation of its resources, technology, and culture

A strategic plan is a statement of how the organization will produce an attractive growth rate and a high rate of return on investment by achieving a market position so advantageous that competitors can retaliate only over an extended time period at a prohibitive cost. This can best be accomplished if the strategic plan allows the organization to innovate in products, processes, and procedures which take advantage of the opportunity, actualize its vision, permit it to compete effectively within its mission, and make it possible for it to reach its goals.

To develop a strategic plan, both the positive and negative implications must be ranked. The strategic plan must encompass all the high-ranked positive implications and avoid or minimize the negative implications of the opportunity, vision, mission, and goals. It must allow enough flexibility within the organization to contain the lower-ranked implications. There should be a strategic statement for every high-ranked implication or cluster of implications.

The process of establishing a strategy does not lend itself well to hard-and-fast, step-by-step protocol. Like many processes discussed in this chapter, it is integrative and holistic. The strategy is best developed in a group setting with a representative sample of the organization participating. When the strategy is complete, review it against the opportunity: It is imperative that the strategy take advantage of the opportunity. Modify the strategy if required.

Sometimes it is advantageous to develop multiple strategies which are then tested with a broader representation of the organization and its stakeholders. This can be done by cycling back and changing one or all of the organization's vision, mission, and goals. The strategy represents the way the organization views the opportunity and is going to take advantage of the opportunity. Eventually a strategic plan must be selected along with a consistent vision, mission, and goals. Sometimes, two areas will be established within an organization with different missions to exploit the opportunity more fully.

When the strategy is complete, an innovation map is created which represents the innovation focus of the strategy. This is done by reviewing each strategic statement, creating a list of innovation implications for each statement, and categorizing each by type of innovation. These can be weighted and combined to create an innovation strategy which is represented by the innovation map.

Compare the innovation map with the opportunity. Do they match? If not, review the process to find out how the discrepancies developed. Determine whether you can alter the strategy to bring it more in line with the opportunity. Using the qualitative terminology we have used throughout this book, if the differences are greater than one level, a way must be found to reconcile them. One-level differences are acceptable, but the organization would better meet the opportunity if all differences were eliminated.

Summary

To develop an innovation strategy, the organization must

- Understand needs and aspirations of people in the organization
- Understand the market in which the business operates
- Understand the needs of its stakeholders
- Synthesize the needs of the market, stakeholders, and people into a vision

- Establish a shared vision
- Develop goals, mission, and strategic plan with the organization
- Create an innovation strategy by interpreting the innovation opportunity through the business needs as stated in the vision, goals, and mission

Caution. Be market driven and remember the customer.

References

1. W. J. Abernathy and K. Wayne, "Limits of the Learning Curve," in *Readings in the Management of Innovation*, M. L. Tushman and W. L. Moore (eds.), Pitman, 1982.

2. Michael E. Porter, *Competitive Advantage*, The Free Press, New York, 1985.

3. Abernathy and Wayne, op. cit.

4. W. J. Abernathy, K. B. Clark, and A. M. Kantrow, *Industrial Renaissance: Producing a Competitive Future for America*, Basic Books, New York, 1983.

5. Ibid.

6. Philip Kotler et al., *The New Competition: What Theory Z Didn't Tell You About Marketing*, Prentice-Hall, Englewood Cliffs, NJ, 1985.

7. Ibid.

6

Assessing
the Organization's
Capacity
for Innovation

There are two key criteria to consider when assessing the organization's capacity for innovation: effectiveness and efficiency. *Effectiveness* is a measure of the alignment of the organization's innovation capability with the opportunity in the marketplace as translated through the strategy. *Efficiency* is a measure of the consistency of focus among all the elements of the organization. Organizations can, depending on their state of development and their degree of focus on the market, exist with various mixtures of effectiveness and efficiency (Figure 6-1).

Effectiveness is being on target most of the time. No person, or organization, can hit the bull's-eye every time. For an archer, effectiveness is having the pattern of shots clustered around the center of the target. The pattern of those shots can be broad or narrow. If the pattern is broad, the archer is not efficient. If the pattern is clustered all together in the bull's-eye, the archer is efficient and effective. If the archer is effective, his or her aim for the target is good, even if the target is moving. If the archer's process of drawing the bow back, aiming, and releasing is consistent, the archer is efficient.

Organizations at their inception are searching for the right combination of effectiveness and efficiency. If an organization works too long to maximize its effectiveness before addressing efficiency, it will not be successful; if it stresses efficiency too soon, it will also not be suc-

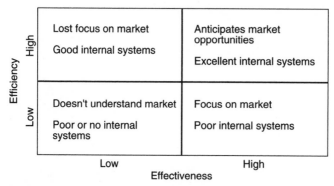

Figure 6-1. Effectiveness and efficiency.

cessful. Therefore, striking the right balance between effectiveness and efficiency is one of the key problems of a start-up organization, maintaining a balance of effectiveness and efficiency is one of the key tasks of a mature organization, and redefining effectiveness and reestablishing efficiency is one of the key problems for a declining organization.

A powerful way to evaluate an organization's effectiveness and efficiency is by examining the type of innovation the organization has a natural proclivity to generate. This characteristic of an organization is similar to its genetic code. An innovation map of the organization's capabilities describes its natural tendency to innovate.

Genetics eliminates some people from playing professional basketball; they simply are not tall enough. For those who can play, genetics is important in determining the position that can be played. Centers are different from forwards who are different from guards. Similarly, there are some organizations that just cannot play in some markets, and those that can play are limited to specific roles. But unlike our genetic makeup, which we can do little about, organizations can, and do, change their natural innovation tendencies—giving them access to new markets, or expanded roles in current markets. The first step to changing an organization's capability to innovate is an assessment of that current capability.

Organizational Elements

Organizations are composed of three major elements:

- Projects
- Resources

■ Culture

The *projects* of an organization are the identified and organized ways that the resources of the organization are applied in order for the organization to reach its goals, and exploit the market opportunities and avoid or minimize the threats. Projects are the way in which the strategy is implemented. Projects can be focused on products, processes, or procedures. They can have the purpose of improving technologies, methods, or materials.

Resources are the "means" of an organization; the resources of an organization are money, people, facilities and equipment, strategic relationships, and intellectual property. The resources of an organization are applied through projects to produce the results required by its strategy and goals.

The *culture* of an organization determines its character; it encourages the development of specific types of resources and the implementation of certain projects. Like social cultures, organizational cultures are known by their artifacts, the things they produce, and the behavior of individuals within the culture. The output of an organizational culture, its products or services, reflects the culture itself.

Figure 6-2 shows a typical anthropological model of a culture. At the core of a culture is its philosophy, how it relates what it believes, values, and acts upon to life. The philosophy gives existence in the culture purpose and meaning. Built upon the philosophy, a culture has a small number of beliefs, things it holds self-evident, beyond questioning. Values are built upon the beliefs, and, therefore, there can be many

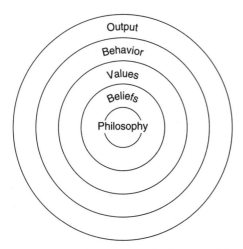

Figure 6-2. Organizational culture model.

more values than beliefs. Values determine the priorities for action, and they become the key factors in decisions. Decisions are made based on what the organization values, and the behavior of people within the culture is based upon their values. There are two different *kinds* of behavior sometimes shown in cultural models. In psychological parlance the term *behavioral norms* describes behaviors that clearly express, as they are directly linked to, the organization's values. Other behavior patterns follow the norms. The output of the organization is its products and services, which have consequences to the organization and its stakeholders, customers and competitors, and society in general.

Dysfunctional Organizations

Organizations become *dysfunctional* when one or more of the innovation capabilities of the elements of the organization (projects, resources, or culture) are not aligned with the innovation opportunity in the market. The organization then is inefficient at what it does. If the organization is ineffective, its products or services will not meet the needs of customers; it will lose market share, and begin to decline. However, an inefficient organization has no such dramatic symptoms. It just struggles with everything it does. It may hang in there, or even decline, depending on the severity of the inefficiencies.

There are six general symptoms of an inefficient organization. No one of these is sufficient in itself to warrant the undertaking of an organizational development program. However, if your organization suffers from several of these symptoms, it may be wise to assess formally the organization's capacity to innovate, and to check the alignment of that capacity with the needs of the market. The following are symptoms of an inefficient organization:

- *Stress and frustrations.* Organizations that have misalignments of the innovation capacity of their resources or culture with their projects have a high degree of stress and frustration. If the people in the organization are better in tune with the needs of the market than the culture allows or the projects dictate, the people will feel stressed and frustrated. If the people are trying to implement the projects but the culture prohibits them from doing so, or it requires a fight each time something is attempted, stress will be obvious.

- *Inappropriate behavior.* Behavior which is inappropriate to the marketplace or the goals of the organization is one indication that the culture may be misaligned with the market. The behavior of many

Navy pilots at Tailhook is an exaggerated example. The culture of the Navy is clearly misaligned with the market (society) they serve.

- *Recurring problems.* The organization may have recurring problems, and the organization may find that quick fixes don't work. This is often caused by a misdiagnosis of the problem; a symptom is observed and a standard solution prescribed. When the solution fails, frustration results. A classic example of this is an organization thinking that its sales force is not responsive enough to customer needs, and prescribing sensitivity training, when in reality the real problem is that the organization's products only partially meet customer needs.

    Quick fixes often fail because the organization has misdiagnosed the problem. And they fail because the quick fix does not have enough flexibility in it to cover the real problem.

- *Requirements only partially met.* For each product or service, there is a set of requirements that must be fulfilled. If the organization's projects, resources, and culture are not aligned, their innovation capacities will also differ. The result of the product commercialization process in this type of situation will fill only a subset of the total requirements, even though all requirements were understood at the beginning. Attempts to fill the remaining requirements after the product is in the market will be extremely painful; an organization with this symptom seems to need continuous proof that additional requirements must be met.

    Sometimes the requirements of the market involve a trade-off between quality, price, and date of availability. Organizations with misaligned projects, resources, and culture have a hard time balancing these in a way appropriate to the market. For example, one large software company we worked with had a new product that the market needed *now*. But the company held it up until the product could meet its own internal defect standards, even though customers told the company that they would tolerate some higher level of defects to get the function right away.

- *Commercialization cycle too long.* When the project, resources, and culture of the organization are misaligned, it takes the organization too long to do *anything*, much less to commercialize a product. With the three elements pulling in different directions, the process slows down as each step becomes a painful excursion.

- *Excessive utilization of external capabilities.* Appropriate use of external capabilities is essential to an organization's success, but if the organization finds itself having to turn to external capabilities on core issues or competencies, then something's gone wrong. The organization may find itself having to partner with other companies too frequently, or having to buy its way out of intellectual property problems. The current national trend toward temporary workers to solve many problems is one example. In one large company, almost all the software developers who possess a critical new skill that is required to meet current market needs come from a temporary agency. This is a clear symptom that the resources are not aligned with the market opportunity.

Assessing the Organization's Capacity to Innovate

Assessing the organization's capacity to innovate requires an analysis of its projects, resources, and culture. This process begins with "customizing" of the definitions of two categories of innovation as shown in Figures 6-3 and 6-4. These are used as guidelines to assess the innovation focus of the projects. Each major project of the organization must be analyzed for its innovation content. This is usually done by a team of people cognizant of the projects, either in a group meeting or by survey. The projects may be weighted as to their significance to the organization and the innovation content scored as shown in Figures 6-5 and 6-6.

The resources are assessed for their capacity to support innovation along a number of different criteria. Each of these must be addressed and their impact on the innovation capacity determined.

Innovation Capacity of the Resources

There are five areas to consider to evaluate the innovation capacity of the organization's resources:

- Money
- People
- Facilities
- Intellectual property
- Strategic relationships

The amount of money available, the patience of the money source, and the return they expect all control the type of innovation possible.

Definitions	Personalization	Examples
Incremental. An innovation which provides modest improvements in performance and/or profitability. Allows goods or services to be produced faster, cheaper, better, more reliably, etc.		
Distinctive. An innovation which significantly improves performance and/or profitability, but is not based on an approach fundamentally different from those presently being used. Typically serves as a foundation for a number of incremental innovations.		
Breakthrough. An innovation based on a fundamentally different approach than those presently being used. Allows one to perform a task that could not be performed at present, or to perform a present task in a markedly improved manner. Typically serves as a foundation for a number of distinctive innovations.		

Figure 6-3. Class of innovation.

There are a number of factors to be considered to determine the innovation capability of the people. First, to determine the class of innovation probable, consider the following:

- Educational level
- Number of areas of expertise per person

Definitions	Personalization	Examples
Product. The product or service provided to customers (external or internal). Examples include improvements in machinery, consumer goods, software, automobiles, etc. These innovations typically involve new and attractive features.		
Process. The way a product is produced or a service is provided. Examples include improvements in internal distribution systems, software programming systems, etc. These innovations reduce lifetime cost of the product/service and improve their quality.		
Procedure. The way in which products/processes are integrated into the operations of the organization. Examples include improvements in advertising programs, repair and maintenance service, and reaction times. These innovations contribute to the customer's comfort in that the product/service is well-supported before and after purchase.		

Figure 6-4. Nature of innovation.

- Length of service with organization
- Communication pattern
- Problem orientation
- Communication type

Number	Weight	Projects	Innovation Type											
			Nature						Class					
			Product		Process		Procedure		Incremental		Distinctive		Breakthrough	
			Rating	Score	Rating	Score	Rating	Score	Rating	Score	Rating	Score	Rating	Score
1														
2														
3														
4														
5														
6														
7														
8														
9														
10														
		OVERALL												

Figure 6-5. Assessing projects.

Rating	Description
O	Little or none of this type of innovation possible. The output of the projects will not reflect this type of innovation.
S	Some of this type of innovation is present. This type of innovation will be barely detectable in the result of the project.
M	A moderate amount of this type of innovation is present. It will be clear to an educated observer of the output that this type of innovation is present.
L	A large amount of this type of innovation is present. It is obvious in the result of the project.
XL	Innovation is a major focus of the project. The results of the project will be recognized for this type of innovative contribution.

Figure 6-6. Qualitative assessment.

- Comfort with risk
- Thinking style
- Innovation style

To determine the nature of innovation probable, consider

- Thinking style
- Focus of thinking
- Thinking entities
- World view
- Skills

There are also numerous factors to be considered for facilities and equipment. To determine the nature of innovation probable, consider

- Buildings
- Pilot lines (test beds)
- Classrooms
- Analysis and test tools
- Design tools
- Manufacturing/development systems

To determine the class of innovation probable, consider

- Buildings
- Offices
- Auditoriums
- Conference rooms
- Pilot lines
- Recreation/exercise facilities
- Communication systems
- Test equipment
- Design tools
- Analysis equipment
- Manufacturing process/assembly equipment

The factors to be considered for intellectual property are

- Patents
- Copyrights
- Trade secrets
- Know-how
- Reports
- Standards
- Specifications

The factors to be considered for strategic relationships are

- Vendors/suppliers/consultants
- Contracts
- Joint ventures
- Cooperative programs
- Strategic alliances

The five elements are combined to create a perspective on the innovation potential of the organization's resources.

Figures 6-7 through 6-11 depict characteristics of some of the elements of the organization's resources that lead to a tendency to produce a specific type of innovation. These can be used to help assess the organization's capacity for innovation. Those elements of the resources not described in Figures 6-7 through 6-11 must be assessed in the same manner as the projects.

Innovation Capacity of the Culture

The culture can be assessed by examining the consequences of its output, the behavior of its people, and the values of the organization. The most effective way to assess the culture is to determine what its values are by making direct inquiries and then check these values against behavior, output, and consequences.

For each of the two parameters of innovation, nature and class, there are different values. The class of innovation is related to the degree of change that the innovation represents. For a culture to produce breakthrough innovation, it must value the type of behavior that is likely to produce breakthroughs, and similar correlations must exist for distinctive and incremental innovation. Because the class of innovation repre-

	CLASS		
	Incremental	Distinctive	Breakthrough
Education level	Low (< BS)	Mid (BS, MA)	High (Ph.D.)
Number of areas of expertise per person	One	Few (2–3)	Many (>3)
Length of service with organization	Long (>15 years)	Mid (10–15 yrs)	Short (>10 yrs)
Communication pattern	Internal	Internal with some external	External & internal
Problem orientation	Internal, narrow	A mixture of both	Pictorial, metaphoric
Risk	Adverse to risk	Some risk taken	Much risk taken
Thinking style	Segmental	Mixture of both	Integrative
Innovation style	Modifying, experimental	Exploring	Visioning

Figure 6-7. Factors to consider to assess the innovation class capacity of people.

		Four Roles of Creative Person				Innovation class
		Explorer	Artist	Judge	Warrior	
Innovation style	Modifying	Works with facts	Procedural puzzle solvers	Based on facts	Soldier	Incremental
	Experimenting	Fact information gathering	Procedural with trial and error	Based on facts and opinions	Team player	
	Exploring	Insightful	New approaches	Intuitive	Questions assumptions dislikes routine	Distinctive
	Visioning	Instinctual	Maximize potential	Goals and mission oriented	Persistent, hard worker	Breakthrough

Figure 6-8. Factors to consider to determine the innovation style of people.

	Nature		
	Product	Process	Procedure
Thinking style	Concrete	Contextual	Abstract
Focus of thinking	Things	Actions	People
Thinking entities	Discrete	Discontinuous	Diffuse
World view	Formism	Mechanism	Organicism

Figure 6-9. Factors to consider to assess the innovation nature capacity of people.

	Class		
Facilities	Incremental	Distinctive	Breakthrough
Buildings	Monolithic, closed	Some openness	Campus, open
Offices	Strongly hierarchical	Somewhat hierarchical	Democratic
	No environmental awareness	Some openness to environment	Openness to environment
	Bull pen	Cubicle	Individual
Auditorium	No	Use cafeteria	Yes
Conference rooms	All centralized	Mostly centralized	Local
Pilot lines	Few, restricted	Some, somewhat accessible	Many, accessible
Recreation/ exercise	None	Some exercise & recreation available	Many, easily available

Figure 6-10. Factors to consider to assess the innovation class capacity of the facilities.

	CLASS		
Facilities	Incremental	Distinctive	Breakthrough
Communication systems			
Telephone	Selective, restricted access	Everyone has phones but access is limited	All, equal access
Message systems	Selective	Some	All
Electronic mail	Selective, internal only	Some have system	All, outside access
Computer conferencing	No	A few have access	Yes
Test equipment	Old generation	Mostly old generation	Latest generation
Design tools	None	Some	Many
Analysis equipment	Behind state of art	Some are at state of art	State of art
Manufacturing process/assembly equipment	Old generation	Some are at latest generation	Latest generation
Pilot line (test beds)	Old generation	Some are latest generation	Latest generation

Figure 6-11. Factors to consider to assess the innovation class capacity of the equipment.

sents the size of change that the organization can support, the values related to innovation class can be thought of as being related to the organization's vitality. For organizations to be vital, they must be alive, growing and changing. The degree of change that the organization can support connotes different types of vitality. No one type, or equivalent set of values, is any better inherently than any other set. It depends on the opportunity and threat in the market, and the organization's strategy. Organizations that are vital may generate all three classes of innovation.

The nature of innovation is related to the quality management system used. The different quality management systems that have been developed over time have a mix of emphases on product, process, and procedure, but each one has a central focus on only one or two of the three. Again, there are no inherently better quality management approaches; which one is most useful depends on the market opportunity and organizational strategy. What is of absolute importance, however, is that the organization pick the correct quality management sys-

| | Innovation nature | | |
Quality concept	Product	Process	Procedure
Jones	shaded		hatched
Deming		shaded	
Juran	shaded		
Ishikawa	shaded	hatched	hatched
Crosby	shaded		
Shuster			shaded
Taguchi	shaded		

Figure 6-12. Correlation of innovation nature encouraged with quality approach. (*Key:* Shaded areas = "strong correlation," hatched = "moderate," and white = "some." See also Figs. 6-14 and 6-15.)

tem for its situation. Mixes of several approaches are also acceptable if the market-driven blueprint is there to follow—otherwise, a mixture is likely to produce mediocre results and confuse the culture. Figure 6-12 shows the approximate correlation between the different quality approaches and innovation nature.

There are ten values related to each of the two attributes of the culture that must be assessed in order to understand the innovation propensity of the culture. These are shown in Figure 6-13. The values of the organization can be assessed by a team of people knowledgeable about the organization, or by a survey of a sample of the people in the organization with an instrument designed to test these values.

Once the values are determined, they must be related to the innovation class and nature. This is done as indicated in Figures 6-14 and 6-15.

The authors have found it useful to use the qualitative scale described in Chapters 4 and 5. In this manner, it is easy to check the innovation capacity alignment among the projects, resources, and culture and their alignment to the strategy. This method provides a pictorial representation of the organization's effectiveness and efficiency.

The result of the assessment is now ready to be converted into three innovation maps. The innovation capability of projects, resources, and culture has been assessed in terms of the six fundamental innovation types. This information will now be expanded to all nine types of innovation.

To fill in an innovation map, use the assessment of the nature of

Vitality (class)	Quality (nature)
Initiative for self-development	Achievement
Peer communications	Workmanship
Environmental awareness	Appropriate technology
Multiple skills	Service
Teamwork	Productivity
Vision of organization's direction	Efficiency
Leadership	Control
Focused creativity	Pioneering progress
Purposeful innovation	Community
Intellectual property	Self-actualization

Figure 6-13. Organizational values for innovation.

Organizational vitality values	Innovation class		
	Incremental	Distinctive	Break-through
Initiative for self-development		▨	▩
Peer communications	▨	▩	▩
Environmental awareness		▨	▩
Multiple skills		▨	▩
Teamwork	▩	▨	
Vision of organization's direction		▨	▩
Leadership		▩	▨
Focused creativity	▩	▨	
Purposeful innovation	▨	▩	
Intellectual property			▨

Figure 6-14. Vitality values correlation with class of innovation. (See Figure 6-12 for Key.)

	Innovation nature		
	Product	**Process**	**Procedure**
Achievement	▨		
Workmanship	▨		
Appropriate technology	▨	▧	
Service			▨
Productivity	▨		▧
Efficiency	▨	▧	▧
Control			▨
Pioneering progress		▨	▧
Community			▨
Self-actualization			▨

Figure 6-15. Quality values correlation with nature of innovation. (See Figure 6-12 for Key.)

innovation as a starting point. Fill in nine types of innovation using the following scheme:

- If class = M, enter rating for nature.
- If class = L, increase rating for nature by one step.
- If class = S, decrease rating for nature by one step.
- If class or nature = O, enter O.
- If class = XL, increase the rating for mature by two steps, with a maximum of XL.

Review the resulting innovation map and adjust values as necessary so that the results are consistent across both rows and columns. Figure 6-16 shows all the combinations possible. Figure 6-17 is an example of a conversion that has already been carried out.

Figure 6-18 shows a blank innovation map of the kind shown in Figure 6-17. Three of these will be required to create the maps for the projects, resources, and culture. The overall ratings of innovation capacity are entered in the columns and rows outside the double-lined box corresponding to the nature and class. Then the method described above is used to calculate and fill in all nine types of innovation.

Innovation Ratings

Nature	Class	Type
XL	XL	XL
	L	XL
	M	XL
	S	L
	O	O
	XL	XL
L	L	XL
	M	L
	S	M
	O	O
	XL	L
	L	L
M	M	M
	S	S
	O	O
	XL	L
	L	M
S	M	S
	S	O
	O	O
	XL	O
O	L	O
	M	O
	S	O

Figure 6-16. Rating conversion chart.

		Class		
		Incre- mental	Dis- tinctive	Break- through
		L	L	M
	Product	S	M	S	O
Nature	Process	L	L	L	M
	Procedure	M	L	M	S

Figure 6-17. Example of a completed rating conversion.

	Class		
	Incre-mental	Dis-tinctive	Break-through

Nature	Product				
	Process				
	Procedure				

Figure 6-18. Blank innovation map for use in mapping projects, resources, and culture.

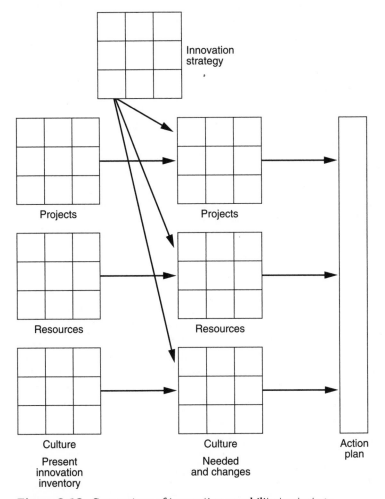

Innovation strategy

Projects

Projects

Resources

Resources

Culture

Culture

Action plan

Present innovation inventory

Needed and changes

Figure 6-19. Comparison of innovation capability to strategy.

Action	Condition	Designate by
Major increase in effort needed	O to XL	++ ++
Strong increase in effort needed	O to XL S to XL	++ +
Moderate increase in effort needed	O to M S to L M to XL	++
Minor increase in effort needed	O to S S to M M to L L to XL	+
No change in effort indicated	The same	0
Minor decrease in effort justified	S to O M to S L to M XL to L	−
Moderate decrease in effort justified	M to O L to S XL to M	− −
Strong decrease in effort justified	L to O XL to S	− − −
Major decrease in effort justified	XL to O	− − − −

Figure 6-20. Guidelines for identifying innovation program needs.

Innovation Capacity

The three innovation maps (for projects, resources, and culture) provide a summary of the innovation potential of the organization. The first thing to look for is consistency. If the three elements of the organization have the same innovation focus, then it is likely that the organization will be efficient. The more dissimilar the focus of innovation is for projects, resources, and culture, the more likely the organization is to be inefficient and hence working in the organization stressful.

The second thing to look for is centrality of focus. Does each innovation map have a clearly defined pattern? Or is it, on the one hand, devoid of any focus? or on the other hand, multifocused? If there is no focal point for the organization, then there is no preferred outcome. Every series of actions in such an organization is just as likely to result in one innovation outcome as another. If there are two areas of focus within the same row or column, then the organization can become schizophrenic unless the areas are adjacent to one another on the innovation map. This can cause stress and conflict within the organization.

The third thing to look at is how similar the three innovation maps are to the innovation map of the strategy (Figure 6-19). If the innovation capacities of the projects, resources, and culture are focused on the strategy, the organization will be effective, assuming that the strategy is focused on the opportunity. Compare the strategy to the projects, resources, and culture. Use the designations in the far right column of Figure 6-20 to indicate the changes required. Enter the results in the three matrices labeled "Needed changes" in Figure 6-19. This is now the basis for an organizational development plan. If there are no (0) or only small differences (+ or −), nothing needs to be done. If the differences are greater, an active organizational developmental plan needs to be developed. A method of developing such a plan will be described in the next chapter.

7

Developing an Organization Which Can Effectively and Efficiently Implement the Strategy

Organizational development is at once simple and complex. Volumes have been written about, degrees are granted in, and professional societies are focused on it. This chapter has the difficult task of converting some of this wealth of information into practical guidelines on developing your organization.

The simple side of organizational development can be summarized in a few sentences: If the key values of the marketplace are known, and these are developed within the organization, the organization will be effective. If the values inside the organization are consistently administered in every decision and program, the organization will be efficient. If the people in the organization naturally support those key values or have a belief structure which will allow them to adopt the values, morale will be high and the people will be motivated to achieve.

The complex side of organizational development is the actual implementation of the simple side. The implementation may take years and is very much a puzzle within a puzzle. Every action or nonaction of management conveys values. Each decision, communication, and action must be weighed against its values content. Values become the ruler against which all organizational strategies, plans, and activities must be measured. And these values do not supplant existing good business practices and measurements. They do, in most cases, help simplify them, but they must overlay them. *Values management* becomes another dimension of management which every member of the management team must learn and practice. Values management is the real battleground of business. It is where the victories will be won over competition and where the challenges of delighting customers will be met. Values management is the key to successful business development.

In the preceding chapters, methods have been developed to aid in understanding the type of innovation, and underlying values, required by the market and accessible to the organization. This chapter will deal with methods of applying the required values to create an organization that will effectively and efficiently develop the appropriate innovations.

Developing Total-Quality Programs in R&D

Quality is an important ingredient in today's global marketplace. Customers expect it, competitors provide it, and technology enables it. Yet so-called "total-quality" programs have had varying degrees of success; they have ranged from being outstanding drivers of total organizational change to being total failures. Reasons for the failures abound but generally can be traced to the use of the wrong quality philosophy for the market, attempts to mix and match from other companies and industries, attempts to do too much too fast, or poor implementation. Of particular concern is the continuing problem of attempting to force what has been learned about quality to date, primarily in manufacturing, into other areas of the organization.

It is thought that research and development (R&D) could benefit from a total-quality approach, but R&D organizations have had only limited success with it. What worked in manufacturing doesn't seem to work in R&D, and R&D professionals resist its implementation. The application of total-quality concepts to R&D is an example of how the concepts of the previous chapters can be applied to organizational development.

Quality Concepts

The definition of *quality* is elusive. It varies between customers in different cultures and between individuals within a culture. What is quality in one application is not quality in another. What constitutes quality in personal transportation is vastly different for an Amish farmer in Pennsylvania, a successful businesswoman in Los Angeles, and Tabitha, a teenage girl in Austin. The customer's definition of quality is contextual, i.e., it depends on the circumstances of the person and the application of the product or service being considered. What a customer considers quality depends upon what he or she values.

If you, as an individual, seek out an artisan or craftsperson to produce something for you, given an accessible, open market, you will seek out someone who has the same values as yours with respect to what is being produced, and has the skills and resources to produce it. In this way, what will be produced will have a higher probability of matching your definition of quality.

We have long since left the age in which artisans or craftspeople produce any significant portion of the goods and services consumed. Organizations have proven to be much more efficient at producing the goods and services needed by mass markets. Where organizations are failing is in effectiveness, i.e., ability to match the values of the customers they would like to serve.

Quality inside organizations has a different "feel" to it. Organizations tend to want to make quality absolute and dictate inside the organization how quality should be created and managed. This creates a conflict between the changing, ethereal nature of quality in the market and the rigid dogmatism of organizations.

Even inside organizations, the concept of quality has changed over

1924	Jones	Quality control—statistical inspection of outgoing goods
1950	Deming	A process which results in satisfied customers
1951	Juran	Fitness for use
1976	Ishikawa	Reduced variance in characteristics
1979	Crosby	Conformance to requirements
1986	Taguchi	Minimal loss to society
1989	Shuster	Relentless individual pursuit of continuous quality improvement

Figure 7-1. Evolution of quality concepts.

1. Create constancy of purpose toward improvement of product and service.

2. Adopt a new philosophy. We can no longer live with commonly accepted levels of delays, mistakes, defective materials, and defective workmanship.

3. Cease dependence on mass inspection. Require, instead, statistical evidence that quality is built in.

4. End the practice of awarding business on the basis of a price tag.

5. Find problems. It is management's job to continually work on the system.

6. Institute modern methods of training on the job.

7. Institute modern methods of supervision of production workers. The responsibility of foremen must be changed from numbers to quality.

8. Drive out fear, so that everyone may work for the company.

9. Break down barriers between departments.

10. Eliminate numerical goals, posters, and slogans asking for new levels of productivity without providing methods.

11. Eliminate work standards that prescribed numerical quotas.

12. Remove barriers that stand between the hourly worker and the right of pride of workmanship.

13. Institute a vigorous program of education and retraining.

14. Create a structure in top management that will push every day on the above 13 points.

Figure 7-2. Deming.

time. While it is difficult to pin down specific dates and people influential in the dynamic development of the concept of quality, it is possible, and instructive, to examine some of the key milestones. Figure 7-1 indicates some of the key milestones in development of quality concepts in organizations. It is important to note that the definition of quality attributed to each individual is only the essence of this person's concept. Each proposes multiple elements of a plan for success, as shown for three of these theorists, Deming,[1] Juran,[2] and Crosby,[3] in Figures 7-2, 7-3, and 7-4, respectively.

1. Build awareness of the need and opportunity for improvement.
2. Set goals for improvement.
3. Organize to reach the goals (establish a quality council, identify problems, select projects, appoint teams, designate facilitators).
4. Provide training.
5. Carry out projects to solve problems.
6. Report progress.
7. Give recognition.
8. Communicate results.
9. Keep score.
10. Maintain momentum by making annual improvement part of the regular systems and processes of the company.

Figure 7-3. Juran.

In the United States, the concept of quality was originated in 1924 at Western Electric, then the manufacturing arm of AT&T. The key was to produce quality telephone handsets. They accomplished this through *quality control,* the statistical inspection of outgoing goods. Since production volumes were so large, they couldn't inspect each telephone, so they relied on sampling procedures. This sufficed until 1950 when Deming, summarized by Dixon and Swiler (1990),[4] went a step back into the business and defined *quality* as a process that will result in a satisfied customer. This is a tremendously powerful concept because it could significantly improve the efficiency of the operation, reduce loss of finished goods, and be proactive rather than reactive.

In 1951, Juran pointed out that it didn't matter how defect-free a product was—that if it wasn't fit for use, it wasn't quality. This is discussed in his book *Juran on Planning for Quality* (1988).[5] A quality buggy whip is no replacement for high-octane gasoline.

Ishikawa (1985)[6] introduced in 1976 some additional concepts of the dispersion of the quality characteristics, pointing out that higher quality would be perceived by the customer if there were less variance in the characteristics. Crosby (1979)[7] introduced the concept of quality as being conformance to requirements. All of us have customers, internal to our organizations and external. If each person in the chain required to fulfill an external customer's need conforms to their customer's requirements, a quality product or service will result. These concepts,

1. Make it clear that management is committed to quality.

2. Form quality improvement teams with representatives from each department.

3. Determine where current and potential quality problems lie.

4. Evaluate the cost of quality and explain its use as a management tool.

5. Raise the quality awareness and personal concern of all employees.

6. Take actions to correct problems identified through previous steps.

7. Establish an ad hoc committee for the zero-defects program.

8. Train supervisors to actively carry out their part of the quality improvement program.

9. Hold a "Zero Defects Day" to let all employees realize there has been a change.

10. Encourage individuals to establish improvement goals for themselves and their groups.

11. Encourage employees to communicate to management the obstacles they face in attaining their improvement goals.

12. Recognize and appreciate those who participate.

13. Establish a quality council to communicate on a regular basis.

14. Do it all over again to emphasize that the quality improvement program never ends.

Figure 7-4. Crosby.

combined with the previous work of Jones and Deming, resulted in concepts such as the Six Sigma Program described by Rifkin (1991).[8]

With the advent of environmental concerns and other issues that roused social consciousness, Taguchi (1986)[9] introduced the concept of loss to society. For every customer need that is filled, there may be some unintended detrimental impact to the rest of society as a result of the method used to satisfy that need. By Taguchi's definition, a high-quality product or service is one that minimizes negative impacts on the rest of society.

In recent years, *total-quality management* (TQM) programs have

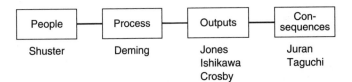

Figure 7-5. Reordered approach to quality.

evolved. The theory behind these includes the concept, as described by Shuster (1990),[10] of quality as the relentless individual pursuit of continuous performance improvements.

The various concepts of quality we have been discussing can be organized under four categories as shown in Figure 7-5:

- People
- Processes
- Outputs
- Consequences

There is a relationship between the four categories: People working together using processes produce outputs which result in consequences to the end user, the producing organization, and society.

Culture

From an anthropological point of view, organizations are cultures. And it is this culture that dictates how effectively organizations produce results. A strong, highly focused culture will result in a very efficient organization. If the focal point of the culture is the market, the organization will be effective. If not, it will produce quality buggy whips instead of high-octane gas.

Cultures are composed of five elements:

- Philosophy
- Beliefs
- Values
- Behavior
- Results

The five are related to each other as shown in Figure 7-6.

At the core of any culture is its philosophy. The philosophy is a

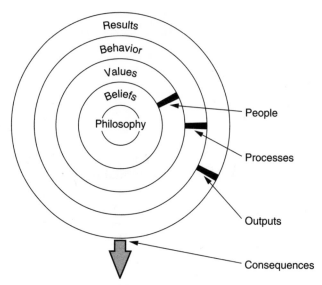

Figure 7-6. Organizational culture.

statement of its rules for success, the formula that has been worked out through years of experience in determining "what works." Beliefs are statements of what the organization believes to be true. Values are based on the beliefs and determine what receives attention; values determine priorities and establish the basis for the behavior of individuals within the organization. Behavior patterns in organizations determine results.

The five elements of culture can be related to the quality concepts as shown in Figure 7-6. The people hold the philosophy, beliefs, and values. Processes are the way people behave with respect to each other and the things they produce. The results of the culture are the outputs, which produce consequences. Thus it is no accident that the pioneers of quality have been, in a piecemeal fashion, mapping out the territory of organizational culture. The choice of which quality concepts to follow has in part been dictated by the time frame in which the organization has operated but also in part by fad. Different philosophies of quality have swept through industry in waves. Some good, even outstanding, results have been obtained when the application of the philosophical approach happily matches the environment in which the organization operates. Lately, it has been fashionable to construct TQM programs in pursuit of a standard or award of some kind or other. In TQM programs, elements in all or many of the quality philosophies have been fitted together. In some cases, companies use benchmarking techniques to determine "best practices" and then cobble all these best practices together.

Suppose you wanted to bake the best possible cake in the world, and you set out to do this by visiting all the famous bakery chefs of the world to determine their most important ingredient. You then proceeded to bake a cake made up of all the critical ingredients of all the master bakery chefs. What would you get? You would get what many quality programs fashioned in this way get, mediocre results that have few if any significant consequences. This blandness pervades the products and services of many organizations. The application of a mix-and-match strategy for quality results in a diffuse culture that can only produce incremental innovations and is confused about the future needs of the market.

Caution. To appropriately develop a TQM program, the focus of the culture must be sharp and on the market.

Quality Fundamentals

To understand the fundamentals of quality it is instructive to look at the roots of the word *quality*. Like many of the words in the English language, it has its origins in the Indo-European language. It began as *kuo*, which was the interrogative. This became *quo* in Latin, also the interrogative: Why? Where? What? When? How? These are all questions of the quality interrogative. Why do it? What are the consequences? What is the output? Where, when, and how are the processes performed? Who are the people?

Quality, then, is the essence of something. Quality is what distinguishes that thing from something else. It is what yields competitive advantage. Therefore, any good quality program must answer all these questions and include elements of each of the four major quality categories. But these elements must be put together in a manner that produces a strong culture sharply focused on the market.

The organization must somehow present itself to the market like the artisan or craftsperson mentioned earlier. It must reflect back to the markets it serves the values of the current and future customers within those markets, and have the right products and the right resources to produce things they want. This is the key to a good TQM process.

Values Management

Values management is an important management tool. The organization must be able to assess the current and future opportunity in the

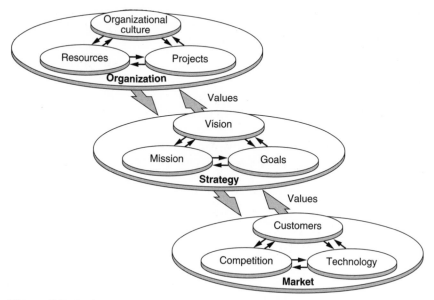

Figure 7-7. Linking organizational culture to the market.

market by determining and forecasting how the needs of customers, responses of competition, and capability of technologies interact with each other and the social, political, economic, technical, and demographic driving forces for change which affect the market. It is necessary not only to translate these into requirements which drive the strategy of the organization but also to transmit values to and through the strategy. The values transmitted by the strategy must then be made inherent in the organization's projects, resources, and culture (Figure 7-7).

Applying Quality Concepts to R&D

The practical application of quality concepts to productive endeavors started in manufacturing and has been refined there. Since manufacturing accounts for 30 to 60 percent of the total cost of the product and delivers the product to the customer through a distribution system, this was appropriate. It is also proper that the focus of the quality programs was on efficiency; there is tremendous leverage in reducing costs and defects in the manufacturing process. It is not appropriate to apply these same quality concepts to R&D, where the financial leverage is different. R&D costs are 5 to 10 percent of the total product costs. Reducing these costs through efficiency, while it may drop through to the bottom line immediately, has little if any positive long-term impact, and has the potential for disastrous negative future impacts. The focus of quality in R&D should be on effectiveness. The leverage here is 10s to 100s of times the R&D costs. A product that matches the requirements and mirrors the values of the customers can produce revenues that dwarf the gains of quality programs in manufacturing. Companies that learn how to apply quality concepts properly in R&D will thus sustain significant competitive advantage.

Implications for R&D Organizations

Quality in R&D should therefore be defined in terms of how well the R&D team has anticipated customer requirements and delivered innovation which delights customers. The research scientist or development engineer must consider more than technology to produce innovation. He or she must be able to see technology as one of three elements of the market their organization operates within, the other two being customers and competition. In addition, this view must go beyond customers, competition, and technology to the environment in which the market operates, the social, political, economic, technical, and demographic driving forces for change that affect how the market is going to evolve over time. To increase effectiveness, the R&D professional must be able to understand these market dynamics and forecast customer needs, technological capabilities, and competitive response. It is only then, because of the length of time that it takes to do technology development and product commercialization, that the professional can produce products that the customer needs. Timing is everything.

As we have stated earlier, R&D must become more effective before focusing on efficiency. Once it does focus on efficiency, the biggest leverage it has will come from the concept of *technology management*. By focusing its energies on a few key strategic technologies, it can become efficient. However, it also must have strategic alliances to be able to meet all needs. Strategic planning of technology and alliances thus becomes a very powerful tool to improve the organization's efficiency.

Utilizing outside sources of technology can be a problem as well. The organization must have effective means of technology transfer. Technology transfer has two major components. The first is communication of the technology, and the second is acceptance of the technology. The first is mechanical, and the second is cultural. To ensure effective and efficient transfer of technology, it is advisable to match the values in the R&D organization to those of the strategic partners.

Technology road maps or some equivalent form of technology management are essential in R&D. It is important to consider three different types of technology: direct, supportive, and enabling. Each of these must be forecasted, and the forecast must not be done in a vacuum but within the context of the market—customers, competitors, and the environmental forces for change. Embedded within this forecasting process is a part of a competitive analysis. The organization must then assess its technological capability against the completed forecast. As noted above, selection of key technologies and the management of strategic alliances to provide other capabilities are essential.

Time and cost of innovation commercialization are only two of the factors important to success. The focus of the innovation effort is also vital. And, the focus of the innovation effort is also different from that in a manufacturing operation.

A focus on not making mistakes is not appropriate in R&D. We know from human nature that we learn by making mistakes. The key to an effective R&D organization is not to reduce mistakes but to minimize the time required to learn from the mistakes and correct the course of action. This can only occur if R&D is linked to the market and the rest of the organization. This can best be accomplished if all are part of a team effort to help make the customer's customer more effective. In many cases, it will be wise also to involve competitors in this "team" through various mechanisms. Collaborative competition involves choosing to collaborate on some elements while reserving others as the basis of competition. Benchmarking is one form this can take. Consortia are another. Technology assessment is another way of determining if you are on track by forecasting technical advance and assessing your organization's position relative to the forecasted advancement.

To focus its innovation efforts, an R&D organization needs a vision, mission, and goals. The vision, mission, and goals are established to take advantage of the future opportunity in the market (customers, competition, and technology), meet the needs of the organization's stakeholders, and fulfill the desires of the members of the organization. A good vision links these three pieces together effectively. The current capabilities—the projects, resources, and culture of the organization—must then be assessed. The difference between the current capabilities and the future desired state must be closed through innovation. R&D must innovate in products, processes, and procedures, and with the degree of innovation (breakthrough, distinctive, or incremental) required to close the gap. This gap defines what the R&D program must be. The R&D strategy maps the route that the organization intends to take from the current state to the future desired state.

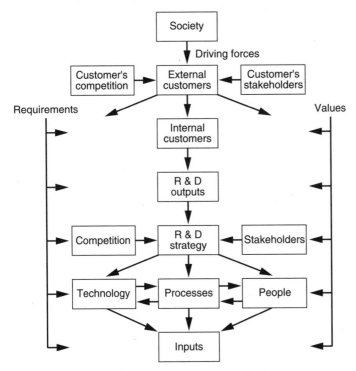

Figure 7-8. Market-driven requirements and values processes.

Establishing a Market-Driven Quality Measurement System

To establish a market-driven quality system in R&D with the appropriate measurements, the consequences must drive the entire process and establish requirements for the outputs, which in turn establish the needs for the R&D lab's processes and people. This in turn places requirements on the input to the entire process (Figure 7-8).

This has significant implications for the lab and the way it views itself. The entire process from input to consequences takes time, and therefore the lab must develop the ability to forecast the future needed consequences for society, external customers, and internal customers. This implies that the R&D lab must be able to understand the driving forces for change in society and how these forces affect the organization's customers. Social, political, economic, demographic, and technical driving forces for change can be identified and provide a multiyear perspective on the evolution of the market the organization serves.

Attempts to shorten the time between input and consequences can

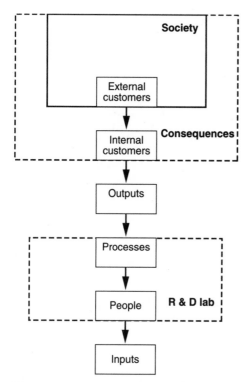

Figure 7-9. Market-driven measurement system.

be valuable because they reduce the need for long-term forecasting which can be difficult. Reduction of the cycle time can also reduce costs. However, an excess emphasis on reducing the cycle time guarantees that only incremental innovations will result. Depending on the market, this may be acceptable. However, in today's environment there are many markets where distinctive, and even breakthrough, innovations are required to delight customers, internal and external, and sustain competitive advantage.

The measurements that an R&D organization chooses to use to evaluate itself must be driven by the market. Figure 7-9 indicates that two sets of conditions must be applied to all measurements. The future requirements of the organization's customers must be forecasted by the organization far enough into the future to allow the R&D organization to produce the innovations in the form of outputs to its internal customers so that it can satisfy customer needs. In order to develop the organization's culture, however, the values embedded in the requirements must also be transmitted, in addition to the traditional requirements of function, form, and cost, throughout the entire process. Each measurement must then be carefully analyzed to determine whether it is encouraging the development of the right requirements and the right values.

Developing a Technically Vital Organization

An organization is vital when it focuses on a few key values which are highly developed; has values which are appropriate to the market and surrounding environment; has consistency of values throughout its projects, resources, and culture; and has values which encourage change and growth. To be vital means to be alive, growing and adapting to the environment.

The term *technical vitality* connotes a special application of this concept of vitality to the technical professionals in an organization. The first application of the concepts in this book took place at IBM's Austin, Texas, site. It was an eight-year program to change the organizational culture of the site to enable the site to cope with and later lead the company in the application of new technology. The site began as a second-source manufacturer of typewriters and is now the lead laboratory for RISC (reduced instruction set computer) workstations and personal computer (PC) operating systems. Following is an account of this development.

Objectives

The requirements for the technical vitality plan and its objectives came from the following 1980 studies:

- A review of several years of opinion survey data and all write-in comments
- A review of several years of "Speak-ups"
- Interviews with key technical professionals and managers
- Review of corporate *technical professional development* (TPD) programs and discussions with TPD corporate staff (including site visits with the director of TPD programs)
- Division executive program review
- Senior site management advice and review
- Support function discussions

- A literature review
- Personal experience as a technical professional and as a manager of technical professionals

Analysis and synthesis of these data resulted in the statement of a set of objectives which remained the same throughout the program.

- Improve image
- Improve communication
- Improve innovation
- Optimize personnel development and education
- Ensure recognition

Image.   First, the technical professional's self-image had to be improved. The technical professional population had, for years, lacked an identity and a strong self-image. This was the result of the organizational culture as it had evolved from its roots, management restrictions on technical professional growth and development, numerous changes to the products and missions, and the lack of an identifiable sitewide shared vision of purpose.

Second, the site's image, as a technical leader in the company, had to be improved. In order to have a broad technology base to fuel technical vitality, the site, in competing for mission, needed to be recognized as having the technical capability to carry out a complex mission. Third, the site, and therefore the company, had almost no presence as a technical leader in the technical world outside the company in the field in which the site specialized. The site published very little in the technical press.

Communication.   First, technical communication systems had to be built and technical communications improved within the site. Then technical communication with the rest of the company had to be improved. The site also had to engage in the free flow of nonproprietary technical and business information in the world outside the company. The site had to build on the development work of others within the site, within the company, and outside the company to reduce costs, avoid false starts, reduce failures, shorten development time, and become a technology leader.

Personnel Development and Education.   Personnel development and education had to be optimized because the site was in a period of rapid, revolutionary change. This fueled an increasing need for education to meet the needs of change and to cause change. Projections showed that the site would not be able to offer all the education that would be required, and methods were developed to improve the effectiveness and productivity of internal education. The largest single factor in potential gains in this area was the technical professional, who had to learn to take responsibility for his or her own development. Teaching technical professionals how to be professional and how to learn was the single most effective thing that could be done. Then, the teaching of process, rather than hard skill, was key to the future of the company.

Recognition. The site had to ensure recognition so that technical professionals who did what was needed became heroes and heroines. Others would then emulate them and those who made contributions would continue to do so.

Innovation. It was clear that creativity was key to the future of the site. Innovation is the commercialization of creativity, and in times of rapid change it is strategically and tactically important. History has shown that companies that establish an innovation-based competitive advantage stay ahead longer. During periods of rapid, revolutionary change, a constant commitment to change is essential. More than a year's worth of study of the barriers to innovation at the Austin site showed the following.

First, pervasive throughout all the studies, there was a very strong desire among the technical professionals to be innovative. They wanted to make change and that was contrary to normal ways of thinking at IBM. Most management, at least most old-line management, believed that people like stability, but that was not what they were saying: they wanted change and they wanted to participate in the change. (People don't want to *be* changed; they want some involvement in the change; there is a significant difference.)

Second, senior management throughout the corporation said repeatedly that they were interested in innovation. That interest was not being transferred down into the organization clearly. The organization didn't have guidelines on innovation, and the people were not really convinced that the company was serious about innovation.

In those cases where management became involved in innovation, that innovation process moved quite a bit faster. What was needed was to convince people that management really was supportive of innovation. What people needed in order to make changes was a sense of security, a sense that it was okay to make change. The only way they could get that was from their management, who needed to reassure them that they really were interested in the change.

Third, the management system that was in place was viewed as a constraint, rather than a support, to innovation. That probably does not come as a surprise to anyone. It is a very difficult, political process to gain acceptance of an idea, and that is not meant negatively. What is meant is that an innovator searches continuously for some coalition of support that will enable him or her to carry the innovation forward.

In general, middle-level management was viewed as unsupportive of innovation programs. Almost universally, the suggestion that came forward was: "Take management out of the innovation process. Provide some sort of bypass to get them out of the way, out of the decision-making process." That was inappropriate; rather, people needed to be convinced that management ought to be in the process and that management ought to support innovation, not find ways to get around it.

Fourth, the formal channels of communication did not significantly impact innovation. There was very weak interorganizational communication—on site, from this site to other company sites, and from the company to outside the company. What everyone says who studies innovation is that free and open communication is the only way that innovations can move ahead more rapidly. It is necessary to get a broad base of information, to get the synergism going that will result in successful innovation. Most people get information from their friends. This is okay, but limits the scope of knowledge that one can have. There are many significant disadvantages to working in a large corporation, but one of the significant advantages is technological sharing; one can build a lot of work on the technological base that exists in the corporation. However, the only way to get at that information is through some of the formal communication mechanisms. People at the site said that two things were inhibiting communication. One was parochialism: people would try to guard information because information is power in an organization as complex as this one. The other was security: people felt that the company's emphasis on security was a detriment to the free flow of technical information.

Fifth, traditional management methods were not necessarily ideal for managing innovation. The company had a very strong emphasis on short-term cost savings. That is not a good way to measure innovation in its early stages. Many times, you cannot determine a return on investment for an innovative idea at its very early stages. You just don't know enough about it. Other tools are needed to help make a decision. This implies that the personality of the innovator becomes more important than the idea because the business cases are not solid. A person who is convincing, who has a strong and dominant personality—or one who has a proven track record—has a greater probability of having his or her ideas accepted and implemented than somebody who has none of those things. Of course, the people who usually have none of these things are the newer people in the organization. So the site was losing ideas from a lot of their young people because they were not allowing them access to the power tools of change. In these studies, we found an example of someone trying to start an innovation who did not have the credentials. He recognized the problem, found somebody who had that kind of experience, brought them into the innovation team, and used that person to help them make the change. The organization needed to employ ways of evaluating ideas other than financially.

Number six was inadequate infrastructure, and we heard many loud complaints about the lack of this support function. There really was none in place to help innovators at the site, and so a lot of suggestions were offered in this particular area. Again, people did not know how to get started. When they did get started, there was nobody there to help, to guide, and to provide the assistance necessary whenever a new idea is started. A new idea is like an infant: it is very susceptible to damage. In its formative stages, you need to have the kind of support system that can help it, enable it to grow a little bit, and then let it stand on its own.

An overarching conclusion was that the environment for innovation in the organization needed to be strengthened. The site needed to create an organizational structure which was innovative. In order to do that a clear vision was required, one that people as well as management shared, one that set direction. The word *vision* implies the power of imagination coupled with unusual foresight. That is the kind of vision that was needed to motivate people and to provide the background and the culture necessary for innovation.

The five program objectives could be met and the process of cultural change facilitated by a focus on four key values:

- Focused creativity
- Purposeful innovation
- Effective peer communication
- Development of intellectual property

Technical Vitality Development Plan

The plan was established in two sections: (1) promotion of corporate programs and (2) development of specific site programs necessary because of the site's unique problems.

The strategy for the development of an Austin Technical Vitality Cultural Change Program was:

- Plan an early, highly visible project.
- Assure an early success.
- Stage the program with quality evident in each new endeavor.
- Develop a phased approach to hierarchy: senior management, technical professional, middle management.
- Treat it as a cultural transformation (five to seven years), have long-term personal commitment, and be persistent and patient.
- Publicize throughout the corporation.
- Solicit voluntary participation from technical professionals.
- Don't add any bureaucracy.
- Keep program ownership in the hands of line management.
- Involve support groups.
- Utilize consultants.

The phased approach to the management hierarchy was considered because of indications as to where the maximum resistance lay. Senior management was clearly supportive of the program, and technical professionals wanted to be involved. The middle management—caught between the demands of the business, the often conflicting desires of senior management, and the constant pressure from the technical professional—was the most reluctant to make changes.

It was clear that this program had to be treated as a cultural transformation. This required patience, with a long-term commitment to change. The elements of a corporate culture—rites and rituals, heroes and heroines, cultural network, and values—were considered in each of the elements of the program.

It was important to publicize such activity throughout the corporation in order to gain support for change. Even if there was no direct line of management control, peer pressure through acceptance and success at other sites was vital to this type of change.

Utilization of support groups and consultants was necessary because of the magnitude of the task and the low level of resources available to the project. This provided an effective lever.

The program to support the corporate plan had three aims:

- Increase awareness of programs.
- Educate in how to use them.

- Establish simple, nonbureaucratic methods for their use.

The corporate programs promoted for utilization at the site were chosen because they supported the four key values. They included

- Continuing education, such as graduate work study, resident study, special study
- Establishment of corporate technical publications
- Sabbaticals
- Technical documentation, for example, technical memos, technical reports, external publications/presentations
- Interdivisional technical liaison (ITL) group: membership, leadership, host meetings (internal professional societies focused on corporate technical needs)
- Corporate technical information center: Current Information Systems (CIS), on-line (computer-based library and publication access)
- Patents and awards
- Technical professional societies: membership, meetings
- Advanced technical positions (high-level technical positions to allow technical professionals to be promoted to nonmanagement sales)

Utilizing the growing knowledge of the site's specific requirements, a series of special programs which emphasized the four key values were initiated to fill the gaps left by the corporate program.

1. *Management emphasis booklet.*   This was a report issued by the lab director enumerating the principles of management he wished line managers to follow. It had a heavy technical vitality emphasis.

2. *Austin Technical Symposium.*   The first program was the Austin Technical Symposium, held in the fall of 1981 with a low budget and mainly volunteer workers. This vehicle was chosen because it had a high probability of success, a high profile, a high level of employee involvement, and a high leverage. The theme was "Creativity—Key to the Future." After the success of the first program, this was institutionalized for every two years. The second symposium had the theme "Creativity—A Key to Productivity." The Austin Technical Symposium was, at its heart, an internal technical professional society meeting. At its core was delivery of 100 to 120 technical presentations on a variety of topics important to the site. The presentations were made by Austin technical professionals and by technical professionals from throughout the global IBM technical community. Executive presentations and consultant talks acted as the focus for the general sessions. Special educa-

tion programs were provided before and after the symposium. Attendance at the symposium was limited to about 400 people, 300 from Austin, because of facilities. Displays of products, technology, and technical vitality programs were open to the entire site. Held on site, it was a high-profile cultural extravaganza that embodied all the values the technical professional culture required.

3. *Monthly seminar series.*   This was a series of consultant and academic speakers that covered a wide variety of topics. The purpose was to bring people into contact with ideas that they might not come in contact with during their normal work. These sessions typically lasted three hours and were attended by an average of 100 people.

4. *Technical magazine.*   The technical magazine, *Creativity,* was developed to establish a communications link to and between technical professional employees. It matured over the years and was widely accepted for its usefulness, content, and readability. It was the precursor of other site newsletters. It was used to affect values, communicate programs, recognize contributions, and educate. It was received by over 50,000 people in other sites and divisions by the end of the program.

5. *Technical library enhancements.*   The technical library was completely revamped, both staff and facilities. The goal was to change it into the type of library necessary during periods of rapid change and to increase its effectiveness.

6. *Special events.*   Two special events were developed: the inventor's dinner and the technical author luncheon. The inventor's dinner, a guest event, was held off site each year to recognize those employees who had contributed to the development of the company's intellectual property. It rapidly became the premier technical recognition event of the site. It helped, among other things, to make the site the per capita leader in inventors among the product sites. The event grew to over 400 invitees and 800 attendees. The author recognition luncheon, also held each year, recognized all the employees who contributed to the technical documentation program of the company.

7. *Special education programs.*   A series of education programs to develop integrative skills for technical professionals was started. Integrative skills were important to the future of the site. The segmentalist approach, necessary for the past environment, is ineffective and will become even more ineffective in the future. The trend had to be reversed and more integrative approaches utilized. Integrative approaches could lead to major cost savings and significant innovations. In addition, the productivity of the technical professional would be markedly improved if his or her perspective were broadened.

Integrative skill development encourages the technical professional in self-development and mastering change. Creativity, innovation, forecasting, professionalism, and leadership are categories of integrative skills. Integrative skills blend technical skills, personal skills, and management skills to facilitate and lead change.

Curriculum Development.   Sixty-six courses and seminars were developed to promote integrative skills. Examples are:

Innovation
- Innovation by Design
- Entrepreneurship Workshop
- Selling Your Innovative Concepts
- Proposing Innovative Concepts
- Gaining Acceptance in Pursuit of Rejection
- Innovation: The Sleeper Awakes

Creativity
- Creative Productivity Workshop
- Creativity Workshop
- Breaking Out of Your Mental Bondage
- Relax Your Way to Improved Creativity
- Creativity Workshop for Managers

Forecasting
- Technology Forecasting Workshop
- The Age of Innovation
- The Strategic Context for Decisions

Leadership
- Managing Change
- Mastering Change
- Change: Opportunity or Challenge?
- Forefronts of Technology

Professionalism
- Managing Technical Vitality
- Staying Alive: Technical Professional Programs for Growth

- Management of Professionals
- Revitalizing Technical Professionals
- Creating a Professional Development Environment

General
- Technical Seminar Series

Program Results

The results of the eight-year-long cultural change program were tracked through a series of surrogate measurements, comparison of performance among sites in the corporation, and subjective evaluations of the site's capability.

Technical reports, i.e., internal formally documented and distributed articles on technical advances, increased over four times. External presentations at professional society meetings and external publications in professional journals increased significantly over the time period. Starting from zero, although cyclical with product commercialization cycles, the number trended upward. Inventions, on a downward trend at the start, took some time to be impacted by the cultural change, which is not surprising if one considers the invention cycle. The number of inventions eventually increased by over 30 percent. The number of site Ph.D. candidates in a corporate-sponsored program also increased dramatically, clearly indicative of changes in attitude both on the part of staff, who applied for the program in larger numbers, and on the part of management, who had to approve the applications. Senior technical staff increased more than sixfold during the program. These were corporate appointments, clearly indicative of the change in stature of the site and its technical people. (See Figures 7-10 through 7-15.)

The technical vitality program at the site was clearly a leader in raising the level of effort on technical vitality throughout the company. Many of the programs were adopted or adapted throughout the corporation, and site personnel acted as leaders in many corporate technical and technical vitality programs.

Changes in the state of the site are difficult to quantify. It has clearly been transformed from a low-technology site with no clear future to a multi-high-technology site with a vital role in the future of the company. It is recognized and promoted as the company's most inventive development and manufacturing site. The RISC technology for advanced workstations is of great strategic importance to the corporation. The development of the programming center, the 1989 commitment to build a software laboratory facility, and the missioning of OS2 to the site is indicative of the company's dependence on the site. Of course, this is not all

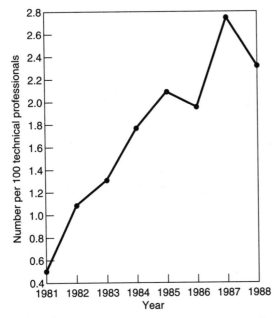

Figure 7-10. A technical vitality program—technical reports.

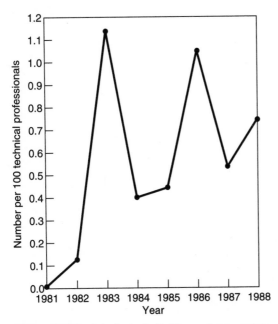

Figure 7-11. A technical vitality program—external presentations.

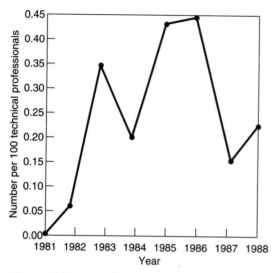

Figure 7-12. A technical vitality program—external publications.

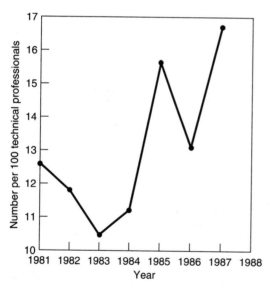

Figure 7-13. A technical vitality program—inventions.

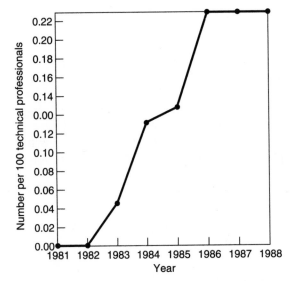

Figure 7-14. A technical vitality program—Ph.D. program study participants.

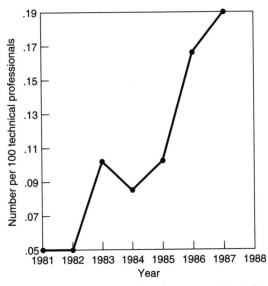

Figure 7-15. A technical vitality program—senior technical staff.

due to the technical vitality program, but the program did create a transformed environment that fed and supported the growth.

The eight-year-long cultural change program at the site to improve its technical vitality was successful. Indicators of vitality have shown marked increases. As noted above, programs have been utilized and duplicated throughout the company. From a handful of people scattered throughout the company who were interested in technical vitality, the company developed a dedicated team of over 50 leaders of cultural change at many sites. And, as also noted above, the site now has a high-technology mission of strategic importance to the corporation.

Creating an Innovative Organization

No matter what the focus of the innovation improvement program is, it must have certain characteristics to be successful.

- It must support the vision, mission, goals, strategies, and plans of the organization.
- It has to emphasize the correct type of innovation.
- It must have a balanced and interdependent use of projects, resources, and culture.
- It has to build on current programs.
- It must be affordable.
- It must employ the appropriate management style.
- It must be capable of being implemented incrementally.
- It must demonstrate early results but be strategically focused.
- It must have built-in sharing of organizational experiences.
- There must be long-term commitment to the program.

These characteristics must be matched up against the characteristics of the program developed. If there is not a match, the program must be changed to have all these characteristics.

Developing an Innovation Improvement Plan

Figure 7-16 depicts the process by which an innovation improvement plan is developed. In the previous chapter, you learned how to assess

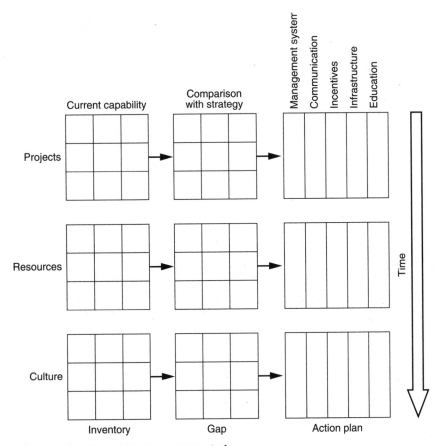

Figure 7-16. Innovation improvement plan.

the innovation capability and focus of the organization through its projects, resources, and culture. Comparison with the strategy results in the identification of specific areas where changes must be made in order to refocus the organization's innovative capability and improve its ability to innovate.

Within the organization there are five fundamental areas to influence and encourage innovation. These are shown in Figure 7-17 as the areas for an action plan. The task you are faced with to implement changes in an organization is to use management systems, incentives, communication systems, infrastructure, and education programs to influence and develop projects, resources, and culture. The easiest to influence is projects; the most difficult is culture. Figure 7-16 shows a time arrow running down through these three areas. While it is impossible to generalize, typically project changes can be effected in large

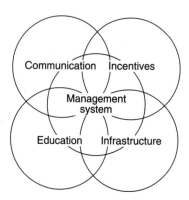

Figure 7-17. Implementation elements.

organizations in one to two years, resource changes can take from two to five years, and cultural changes take over five years. This means that your strategic perspective must have at least a five-year horizon to effectively utilize the organizational culture you have developed. If you must change a large organization in less than five years, it is probably wise to consider other ways of developing an organization such as starting a new company, acquisition, or joint venture.

The five areas, or elements, are interdependent and overlapping as shown in Figure 7-17. As you can see, it is the management system that holds it all together. The five areas were defined in Chapter 6 and will be discussed again below.

Incentives are programs, formal and informal, which recognize, reward, and encourage members of the organization to be innovative. *Communication systems* are both informal and formal ways to facilitate the free flow of information within the organization. They also exist to facilitate the interchange of information with the world outside the organization. *Education programs* are put in place to train and educate members of the organization. They exist to develop skills, ability, and knowledge in four areas, technical, personal, management, and integrative, as shown in Figure 7-18.

Integrative skills are generally overlooked by organizations. Quite often thought to be "soft," they are bypassed for the "harder" skills like learning how to design an integrated circuit. However, in today's environment, and especially when trying to encourage innovation, they are essential. They actually should be emphasized by the organization over technical skills, which individuals can be expected to develop on their own. Integrative skills fall into categories such as innovation, creativity, forecasting, professionalism, and leadership.

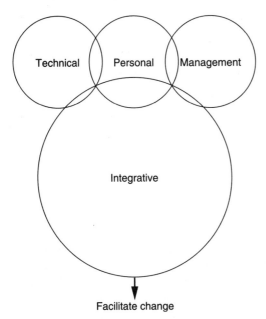

Figure 7-18. Education programs.

Infrastructure refers to the formal structures that facilitate the operation of the organization. This covers business structures that organize activities and provide a hierarchy of control and responsibility. Some business structures are listed in Figure 7-19. *Management systems* refers to the formal and informal programs that management uses to manage and monitor performance of the organization.

Working with these five elements of the organization, the innovation action plan is devised. It has three steps:

- Make changes in projects.

  Enhance those needed.

  Deemphasize those not needed.

  Create incentives, education, communications, infrastructure, and management systems which reinforce the project changes.

- Support project mix change with changes to resources by creating incentives, education, communications, infrastructure, and management systems which encourage appropriate resource development.

- Ensure effectiveness of project mix change and resource change through changes in organizational culture. Again, this is implement-

- **Technical center**
  - Advances state of the art in company/industry
  - Focus on materials and methods/tools of fabrications
  - Upgrading/replacement materials/practices
  - Lower-cost manufacturing
  - Improve performance

- **Research center**
  - Basic research
  - Applied research

- **New-products center**
  - Enriches product line of existing business within a company
  - Innovative features to existing products
  - Utilize existing technologies
  - Conform to existing product functions
  - Exploit existing marketing channels

- **Captive R&D**
  - Addresses needs of a single business entity in a company
  - Single or few missions
  - Can include:
    - Basic research
    - Applied research
    - Improved product design
    - New business ventures (skunkworks)

- **External teams**
  - Service oriented
  - Contract R&D
  - Universities/consultants/companies
  - Government-supported centers

Figure 7-19. Business structures relevant to innovation.

- **Internal ventures center**
  - Strategic business unit (SBU)
  - Independent business unit (IBU)
  - Incubator
  - Skunkworks

- **External ventures center**
  - Product or business oriented
  - Acquisition
  - Establishment of minority position
  - Joint venture

- **Licensing arrangements**
  - Fill gap
  - Shorten time to market
  - Maintain technical dynamism of an industry

Figure 7-19. Business structures relevant to innovation. (*Continued*)

ed by incentives, education, communications, infrastructure, and management systems which encourage the development of the appropriate culture.

This chapter will cover these three steps of organizational change. In essence, your task, in order to effectively implement organizational changes, is to complete the matrix shown in Figure 7-20.

Project Improvement Plan

The project improvement plan is developed in four steps:

- Review the innovation gap for projects, i.e., the difference between the capability and strategy.
- Identify the projects that are contributing to the gap.
- Change the project mix to support the innovation strategy by building on the current mix.

Action area	Projects	Resources	Organization culture
Incentives			
Communication			
Education			
Infrastructure			
Management system			

Figure 7-20. Organizational improvement plan.

- Make necessary changes to the implementation elements to enable the altered project mix.

  Management systems
  Communication
  Incentives
  Infrastructure
  Education

Resource Improvement Plan

The resource improvement plan is developed in three steps:

- Review the innovation gap for resources needs.

- For types of innovation where change is needed,

  Determine the reason for needed change.
  Alter those elements of the resources which contribute to the needed change.

- Make the necessary changes to the implementation elements to enable the altered resources.

  Management systems
  Communication
  Incentives
  Infrastructure
  Education

An example of a resource improvement plan is shown in Figure 7-21.

In the example in Figure 7-21, the resource categories which needed help were the people, facilities, and equipment. Improvement was

Innovation resource	Innovation gap	Reason	Action	Area
People	Breakthrough process	Education level	Patent process	Infrastructure
		Thinking style	Encourage participation in process-oriented professional societies	Communications
			Reward for process implementation	Incentives
			Increase education level	Education
			Teach integrative skills	Education
			Develop process measurements	Management systems
Facilities/ equipment	Breakthrough process	Pilot lines	Set up internal venture	Infrastructure
			Establish computer conference	Communication
			Develop education program to support new pilot line	Education

Figure 7-21. Example of a resource improvement plan.

needed in one type of innovation—breakthrough process. In looking at the assessment of innovation capability of the organization, it was determined that the reasons for the innovation capability not matching the strategy had to do with education level, thinking style, and pilot lines. In this case the five areas were reviewed for potential programs that might help build the specific type of innovation required and fix the identified problems. The column labeled "Action" is the result of this process. Several programs are suggested which would help this organization improve its ability to produce breakthrough process innovations.

Organizational Culture Improvement Plan

As we have noted before, there are four basic elements of an organizational culture: values, heroes and heroines, rites and rituals, and an informal communication network.[11] These are shown schematically in Figure 7-22.

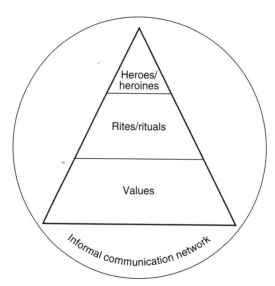

Figure 7-22. Elements of organizational culture.

The *values* of an organization are its bedrock; they are fundamental. They determine the characteristics of the culture and the people in it. They determine what will work and what won't. Values determine the priority of attention and action within the organization.

Rites and rituals are the way the values become institutionalized. They are embodied in the informal and formal methods by which work is accomplished. They span the range from the informal manner of greeting visitors to the formal planning process.

Heroes and heroines personify the values. Values are difficult to comprehend. People who make the values real by their actions become the heroes and heroines of the organization.

The *informal communications network* holds it all together with stories about the heroes and heroines.

It is the role of management to determine the value set that the organization must have for success. Then it is the manager's role to ensure that no inconsistent messages are sent into the organization through the identification of heroes and heroines, implementation of rites and rituals, and selection of stories that are passed around.

It is important to have a strong, simple, and consistent culture. It has been shown that organizations with strong cultures are much more likely to succeed than those with weak or unfocused cultures.

Organizational culture is also important to people in the organization for the following reasons:

- People know how to behave.
- People feel better about what they do.
- Better decisions are made.
- The culture directs innovative activities.
- The culture can support needed project and resource changes.

The important characteristics of culture are:

- There is no "absolute right" corporate culture.
- Companies with a strong corporate culture are more likely to be successful.
- There is a best organizational culture for the situation.
- The organizational culture controls the amount and type of innovation in an organization.
- A balanced, strong organizational culture with mechanisms for culture change is essential in today's environment.

What are some of the elements of a culture which promotes innovation?[12] It is not category conscious. It encourages the continuous creating of teams with new and different configurations. The culture encourages problem identification by its members. It has looseness of boundaries so that people can envision new and intriguing projects. It has virtually unrestricted communication for its projects and for the discussion of alternatives to anything it does. The people have a sense of unity and identification with the whole, with mutual respect, participatory teams, multiple ties across the organization, and off-job socializing. This type of culture is guided by the future. It has investment-centered rewards rather than payoff-oriented rewards. Individuals and teams are not contradictory concepts. Job assignments are broad, ambiguous, nonroutine, change-directed, and overlapping. It generally has complex organizational relationships. Members of the organization have pride. There is a great deal of mobility for its people. Excitement is everywhere. The people are excited about what they are doing.

To develop a culture which promotes innovation it is necessary to

- Encourage a culture of pride

  By highlighting achievements through visible rewards
  By applying innovation from one area to another

- Enlarge access to power tools for innovative problem solving
- Improve lateral communication

By bringing departments together
By exchanging people
By creating cross-functional links/overlaps
By team formation for tasks

- Reduce unnecessary layers of hierarchy

    By removing barriers to resource access
    By lowering decision authority

- Increase information about company plans

- Take advantage of the capacity of people

The culture improvement plan is focused on values. There are six steps:

- Determine values needed to fill innovation gap.

- Determine current values.

- For each value that needs changing or for new values needed, develop a cultural change plan.

- Consider heroes/heroines, rites/rituals, and cultural network.

- Establish culture that best meets type of innovation required.

- Develop through implementation elements.

    Management system
    Communications

Implementation elements	Cultural elements		
	Heroes/ heroines	Rites/ rituals	Informal communication network
Management system			
Communication			
Incentives			
Infrastructure			
Education			

Figure 7-23. Cultural values development plan—defining the task.

Incentives
Infrastructure
Education

Your task in developing a cultural change program is described in Figure 7-23. You must identify for each value that needs improvement a series of actions in each of the three cultural elements in some or all of the implementation elements.

An example of a value development plan is shown in Figure 7-24. As in the previous example involving resources, the values needed are those that will promote development of breakthrough processes. The figure indicates the type of action that could be taken in some of the areas to develop this type of value in the organization.

Innovation type	Organizational culture element	Actions to develop needed values	Implementation element
Breakthrough process	Heroes/heroines	Use person who has demonstrated breakthrough process capability as an internal consultant.	Infrastructure
		Establish internal professional society on process with leader who has demonstrated capability.	Communications
		Set up special project for person who demonstrates capability and give freedom to pursue interests.	Incentive
Breakthrough process	Rites/rituals	Junior members of staff serve an apprenticeship with hero or heroine.	Infrastructure
		Set up weekly seminar.	Education
		Establish special award ceremony.	Incentive
		Establish periodic review meeting.	Communications
Breakthrough process	Informal communication network	As successes occur, build on and pass stories into organization.	Communications

Figure 7-24. Example of a cultural values development plan.

Summary

You have now completed the market-driven innovation process. You started by determining the innovation opportunity in the marketplace. Then you developed vision, mission, and goals which not only met the needs of the marketplace but also met the needs of business and the people in the organization. This helped you to develop an innovation strategy to take advantage of the opportunity. Then you assessed the innovation capability of the organization, compared it with the strategy, and created an innovation improvement plan to help your organization effectively implement your innovation strategy.

This has been described as a linear process for simplicity, but only rarely does it stay a linear process. In the real world there are loops, feedback, and diversions. It is important, however, to keep the structure in mind and to keep returning to it. This process will serve you well at solving complex problems you face if you use it to organize your thinking and actions. A different, more integrated, view of the concepts is shown in Figure 7-25.

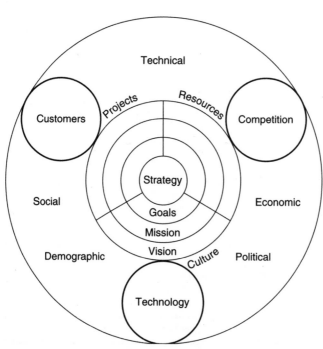

Figure 7-25. Market-driven innovation—an integrative view.

References

1. George Dixon and Julie Swiler, *Total Quality Handbook*, Lakewood Books, Minneapolis, MN, 1990.

2. J. M. Juran, *Juran on Planning for Quality*, The Free Press, New York, 1988.

3. Philip B. Crosby, *Quality Is Free*, McGraw-Hill, New York, 1979.

4. Dixon and Swiler, op. cit.

5. Juran, op. cit.

6. Kaoru Ishikawa, *What Is Total Quality Control?* Prentice-Hall, Englewood Cliffs, NJ, 1985.

7. Crosby, op. cit.

8. Glenn Rifkin, "Pursuing Zero Defects under the Six Sigma Banner," *The New York Times*, January 31, 1991, p. F9.

9. Genichi Taguchi, *Introduction to Quality Engineering: Designing Quality into Products and Processes*, Kraus International Publications, Tokyo, 1986.

10. David H. Shuster, *Teaming for Quality Improvement*, Prentice-Hall, Englewood Cliffs, NJ, 1990.

11. Terrence E. Deal and Alan A. Kennedy, *Corporate Cultures*, Addison-Wesley, New York, 1982.

12. Rosabeth Moss Konter, *The Change Masters*, Simon and Schuster, New York, 1983.

8

Growing a Company

Going Global with Acer

Observations

Acer is one of Taiwan's most successful high-technology companies. It is a prime example of how to "grow" a company.

In 1986, the management of Acer, led by Stan Shih, made a series of decisions which were extremely important to the future of Acer. Acer developed a strategic plan in 1986 that called for it to become a $1 billion company in five years, an incredible goal considering that Acer's annual revenue at the time was $154 million.

In 1991, just as Acer was about to reach its goal, the authors made an analysis of Acer's strategy and implementation plan using the market-driven innovation methodology. This retrospective analysis affirmed the correctness of the Acer strategy. It showed that the strategy was very much in line with the market opportunity. However, the innovation capability of the organization in 1986 did not match the strategy in all aspects.

The innovation capability of the culture of the Acer organization was very much in line with the strategy. Acer was a company that had been built by Stan Shih and his four cofounders from the ground up. The organizational culture was a reflection of the values of the founding management team. As this team, together with other top management, developed the strategy, its no wonder that the culture was consistent with the strategy.

However, the innovation capabilities of the resources and projects of

149

the organization differed somewhat from the capabilities required by the strategy. The people who constituted the resources of the company were technical people who liked to make a significant technical contribution. It's not a surprise that they would be more inclined to distinctive and breakthrough product innovations than to the incremental product innovations required by the strategy. Also, the strategy called for significant procedural innovations, something that the technical people of Acer were not skilled at. The project focus tended to follow the desires of the people, and the constant attempts to correct back to the strategy probably caused some tension.

Acer management realized instinctively that there were some deficiencies. As a result, they brought in people from the outside at high levels in the company to augment the resource capability. This was a bold new step for Acer. Management before had always been developed from within. This step was not taken well by the people, who referred to the outsiders as "parachuters." While this action was necessary for Acer's ambitious plans, it damaged the corporate culture, which in 1991 was still being repaired.

Introduction

Acer started in Taiwan in 1976, under the name of Multitech, with five cofounders and a paid-in capital of $25,000. In the beginning, Multitech provided engineering design services to electronics companies in Taiwan. Later it started to represent companies, mostly from the United States, in the fields of electronics, computers, and integrated circuits, in addition to other trading activities. When the Hsin-Chu Science-Based Industrial Park was opened in 1980, Multitech was one of the first companies to join the Park in the business of personal computers (PCs). With hard work from all its employees, coupled with leadership and the booming world economy, Multitech grew steadily. In 1986, at the tenth anniversary of the company, it had become the leading high-tech trading firm and the largest computer manufacturer in Taiwan. The growth rate was 88 percent from the previous year. The revenue was $154 million with approximately 2200 employees. Though its business had expanded to over 70 countries in the world, Multitech was basically a Taiwanese company. But it was poised to go global.

In May of 1986, Multitech launched a major activity in preparation for its globalization. It spent close to six months involving all levels of people in management and technology to develop a five-year plan. The most significant items of the five-year plan were

- Globalization
- A $1 billion revenue objective for 1991
- Average return on equity (ROE) greater than 25 percent
- Productivity improvement better than 15 percent per year

Many activities were put in place to achieve the goals of the five-year plan. The revenue goal of $1 billion for 1991 was made public to put the company in the limelight of the business world in Taiwan. With its success every year in the following five years, it soon became a major computer supplier in the world market. By the end of 1991, the company achieved the goal of $1 billion in revenue and was on its way to becoming a global company.

Strategic Planning

In 1986, Multitech's strategic planning for the following five years indicated the following:

- Brand name and distributors and original equipment manufacturers (OEMs) are of equal importance as customers.
- World market distribution was set at approximately one-third for the United States, one-third for Europe, and one-third for the rest of the world.
- Future distributors will be qualified.
- Every division and location of the company will have specific goals and objectives which are consistent with the goals and objectives of the company.
- The company will be growth oriented.
- Company stock will be traded openly on the stock exchange of Taiwan.
- Globalization is a must.
- Joint ventures and acquisitions will be actively pursued.
- The corporate culture shall be strengthened with common vision.
- Products of the company will be mostly "followers" with only occasional "stars" and "leaders."
- The production facilities will be optimized with a combination of automation and manual operations.
- Standard and current technologies will be used for the products.

- It is understood that the market windows for products will be very narrow.
- Quality will be designed in.

Action Plans

Many actions were planned and executed by the company during the five years from 1986 to 1991. Some of the more important ones are listed below.

- *Name change.* This was the most daring and important action that the company took. It was also the most difficult decision for top management to make. However, the name change to Acer has been very successful.
- *Intellectual property rights (IPR).* Great emphasis was placed on IPR through communication, education, and incentive programs in the company. The purpose was to make people more aware of the importance of IPR in business. It taught people to:

  Respect the IPR of its competitors.
  Actively develop its own IPR.
  Help create an image that Acer was of global stature.
- *Globalization through localization.* One of the major activities in this category was the recruiting of international executives, mostly in the marketing area, to manage operations in the United States, Japan, England, and other countries.
- *Acquisitions and joint ventures.* Acer acquired companies and/or formed joint-venture companies in Taiwan, in the United States, in Japan, and in Europe. These activities were mainly for the purpose of establishing marketing channels and acquiring technologies and products. Some manufacturing facilities were also established either as joint ventures in Taiwan or wholly owned subsidiaries outside Taiwan.
- *Going public.* Acer went public in November 1988, as planned. It was a major change for the company to seek capital from the public—instead of generating capital only from within as it had for so many years—to fund its many globalization activities.
- *Formation of independent business units.* Acer went through a major reorganization to form several *independent business units* (IBUs). This was done to streamline operations as well as to give current products importance and emphasis equal to that of future products.

Most of the R&D engineers were more interested in activities related to the future products because they were usually higher-technology projects, and in some cases involved leading technology. They thought these were more challenging, and were less enthusiastic about innovation activities in the current products which although they had a lower level of technology were the major revenue producers of the company. With the proper education, communication, incentive, and management systems, Acer was able to shift the R&D resources and projects to balance activity between incremental and distinctive innovation.

Analysis

What follows is a retrospective analysis of the major growth phase of Acer as it went from being a Taiwanese company to a global force in personal computers. The analysis indicates why the strategy and plans of Acer were successful and why this period left Acer with some unresolved issues that became problems as the company transitioned to its next phase of development.

Customer Needs

Computer products were sold through two different channels before they reached the end users. For this reason, in this analysis, the customers of Acer were not considered to be the end users but these two channels:

- Distributors
- OEM companies (original equipment manufacturers)

The distributors' needs were items such as

- Price
- Reliability
- Quality
- Support
- Spare parts
- Financial terms
- Timeliness
- Flexibility

- Marketing
- Documentation

The OEM customers (companies) were interested in items such as

- Quality
- Price
- Schedule
- Design capability
- Documentation

Clearly some needs were common to both distributors and OEMs. The nature, class, and strength of the needs are shown in Figures 8-1

Item	Nature	Class	Strength
Price	P1, P2	I	L
Reliability	P1, P2	I	L
Quality	P1, P2	I	L
Support	P3	I	M
Spare parts	P1, P2	I	S
Financial terms	P3	D	M
Timeliness	P2, P3	I	L
Flexibility	P2, P3	D	L
Marketing aid	P3	I	M
Documentation	P3	I	L

The notations are:

P1: Product
P2: Process
P3: Procedure
I: Incremental
D: Distinctive

BT: Breakthrough (this item does not appear here but will later).
L: High importance (low)
M: Medium importance
S: Low importance (small)

Figure 8-1. Distributor's needs (current customers).

Item	Nature	Class	Strength
Quality	P1, P2	I	L
Price	P1, P2	I	L
Schedule	P2, P3	I	L
Design capability	P2	I	M
Documentation	P3	I	L

Figure 8-2. OEM companies' needs (current customers).

and 8-2. The first need, price, is shown with an innovation nature of P1 (product) and P2 (process), indicating that, from the distributor's viewpoint, price was associated mainly with the innovation activity in product and process. The price is shown also with an innovation class of I, indicating that, to the distributors, the price was associated mainly with incremental innovation activity. Price is shown also with a strength of L, indicating that it was of large importance to the distributors.

The financial terms that the distributors were interested in are shown with an innovation nature of P3 (procedure), indicating that, to the distributors, the financial terms (how and when the distributors should pay Acer for the products and services they received from Acer) were associated with procedure innovation activity. It also shows that financial terms were of a D (distinctive) class with a strength of M, or of medium importance to them.

As we can see in Figure 8-2, for OEM customers, since they were computer manufacturers themselves, quality was of the highest importance. While the design capability was of medium importance to them, the delivery schedule of the products was very important because it was tied to their own product announcement schedule.

The nature, class, and strength of the needs of identified potential customers are listed in Figures 8-3 and 8-4. If we compare these figures with the previous two figures for current customers, the difference is clearly shown in the shift in class. While in most of the needs categories the current customers required incremental innovations, in most needs categories the identified potential customers required distinctive innovations—the reason being that the identified potential customers, who were customers of Acer's competitors, needed a distinctive innovation, something clearly different, to become Acer's customers.

Item	Nature	Class	Strength
Quality	P1, P2	D	L
Name	P3	D	L
Support	P3	D	L
Price	P1, P2	D	L
Flexibility	P2, P3	I	M

Figure 8-3. Distributor's needs (identified potential customers).

Item	Nature	Class	Strength
Satisfy need	P1	D	L
Design capability	P2	D	M
Quick response	P3	D	L
Quality	P1, P2	D	L

Figure 8-4. OEM companies' needs (identified potential customers).

Item	Nature	Class	Strength
Name	P3	BT	L
Quality	P1, P2	D	L
Price	P1, P2	BT	L
Support	P3	D	L

Figure 8-5. Unidentified potential customer needs.

The items of interest to the unidentified potential customers are listed in Figure 8-5. The unidentified potential customers were those who were not known to Acer in 1986. They also did not recognize Acer's products and most likely would not even know the company. For those unidentified potential customers to become Acer's customers,

	Incre-mental	Distinctive	Break-through
Product	L	L	S
Process	XL	L	S
Procedure	L	L	S

Figure 8-6. Summary innovation map for customer needs.

the class of innovation activity would have to be raised even higher, to distinctive, and perhaps even to breakthrough.

The summary innovation map shown in Figure 8-6 indicates that

- Overall, the customers required very little in the way of breakthrough innovation activities for product, process, and procedures.
- The innovation activities with large interests were of incremental and distinctive class.
- Extra-large incremental innovation activity was required for process.

Technological Capability

Technologies were classified as direct, supportive, and enabling. For the computer business that Acer was engaged in, the major items of interest in the three classifications were

- Direct technologies

  Microprocessors
  Memory
  Storage
  Display
  Input
  Output
  Power supplies
  Software

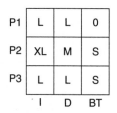

	I	D	BT
P1	L	L	0
P2	XL	M	S
P3	L	L	S

Figure 8-7. Innovation map of technological capability.

    Operating system, diagnostics
    Packaging

- Supportive technologies

    CAD/CAM
    ASIC (application-specific integrated circuit)
    Manufacturing process
    Auto-warehouse
    Testing (reliability, burn-in, FCC (Federal Communications Commission), UL (Underwriters Laboratories))
    Development process
    Quality

- Enabling technologies

    System architecture
    New microprocessors

A technology innovation map was constructed by the same method as the customer needs innovation map. The nature (P1, P2, or P3), class (I, D, or BT), and strength (L, M, or S) for the direct, supportive, and enabling technology capabilities were assessed. The technology innovation map is shown in Figure 8-7. It indicates that

- The innovation capabilities for products were largely of incremental and distinctive classes. No innovation capability seemed reasonable in the breakthrough class.

- Extra-large innovation capability was seen in the incremental class for process.

Competitive Response

For Acer the three types of competitors—direct, indirect, and structural—were as shown in the table on the next page.

	Type of competitor	
Direct	Indirect	Structural

■ Multiproduct companies
IBM
Unisys
Texas Instruments
Hewlett-Packard
Bull
NEC
Toshiba
Canon
ICS
  Etc.
 	
■ PC companies
Apple
Compaq
Dell
Everex
  Etc.
 	
■ Others
Commodore
Radio Shack
Other Taiwan PC companies
	■ Minicomputer companies
	
	■ Word processor, calculator, fax machine manufacturers
	
	■ Networked large-systems manufacturers
	
	■ Teleconferencing equipment manufacturers
		■ Unknown (No important structural competition could be seen, using a five-year time horizon.)

The innovation map for competition was constructed and is shown in Figure 8-8. It indicates that

■ No competitor was focusing innovation activity in breakthrough.

■ Competitive innovation activity was extra large for products of an incremental class.

■ Competitors also focused largely on distinctive procedural innovation activity.

Market Opportunity Analysis

The customer, technology, and competition innovation maps were then combined into a market opportunity innovation map as shown in Figure 8-9. There are no rigid rules for combining the three innovation maps into one. Common sense and sound judgment must be used to synthesize customer requirements, technology capability,

	I	D	BT
P1	XL	M	0
P2	S	M	0
P3	S	L	0

Figure 8-8. Innovation map for competition.

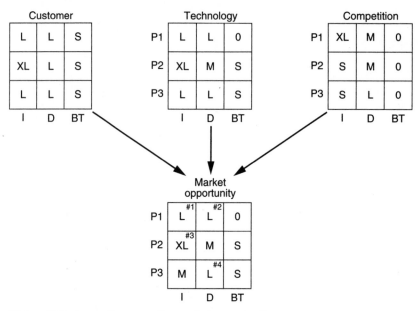

Figure 8-9. Innovation map for market opportunity.

and competition's response. The idea is not to focus on the mechanics but rather on the knowledge which can be used to make better decisions.

The mechanics of the synthesis process can be illustrated by considering the four points in the market opportunity innovation map labeled 1, 2, 3, and 4.

Point 1. For incremental product innovation, large was chosen for the market opportunity innovation map for the following reasons:

- Customers' needs were large, technological capability was large. Needs were matched by technological capability.

- Even though the competition's response was extra large, it made no sense to raise point 1 to extra large to match the competition because the capability of technology and needs of customers were still at the large level. Therefore, large was chosen. This is a competitive threat which was ignored because it did not seem to warrant the level of effort required to match all competitive responses.

Point 2. For distinctive product innovation, large was chosen for the market opportunity innovation map for the following reasons:

- Customers' needs were large, the technological capability was large, so they were again consistent.

- The competition's response was medium, a lower activity level than the large needs. Large was therefore chosen. This is a competitive opportunity.

Point 3. For incremental process innovation, extra large was chosen for the following reasons:

- Customer's requirements and the technology capability were again consistent.

- The competition's response was small. An extra large indicates a significant opportunity for competitive differentiation.

Point 4. For distinctive procedural innovation, large was chosen for the following reason:

- Customers' needs were large, and technological capability and competition's activity level were also large.

Strategy Innovation Map

The strategy of Acer was analyzed for its innovation content. The strategy innovation map was constructed accordingly and is shown in Figure 8-10. It indicates that

- Most of the significant innovation activities were of incremental class.

- No innovation activities were planned in breakthrough.

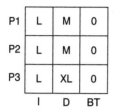

Figure 8-10. Strategy innovation map.

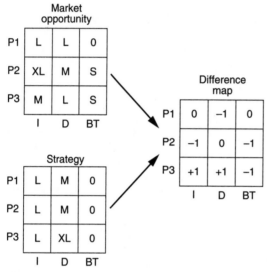

Figure 8-11. Difference innovation map.

- An extra-large amount of innovation was planned for distinctive procedure innovation. This was due mainly to the emphasis on globalization.

The market opportunity innovation map was then compared with the strategy innovation map shown in Figure 8-10. The "difference" map shown in Figure 8-11 was constructed by simply taking the difference between the two maps. A plus sign indicates that the corporate strategy in that particular category called for more innovation activity than the market opportunity required. A minus sign indicates the opposite. A zero indicates that the strategy and the market opportunity in that particular category were aligned. A zero is the ideal case. A difference of 1, whether plus or minus, is not considered significant and should not be a cause for alarm. In this example for Acer, the difference map shows that the corporation's strategy and the market opportunity were basically aligned in all areas.

If, however, 2s or 3s were observed in the difference innovation map, it would have been a warning that the corporate strategy was not meeting the requirements of the market opportunity. A company with this problem would most likely not be able to take advantage of the market opportunity unless it chose to alter the strategy to align it with the market opportunity. Market-driven innovation methodology provides a warning signal which is most useful in the early stages of the strategic planning cycle.

Acer's difference map showed only 0s and 1s, a good indication that the corporate strategy was aligned well with the market opportunity and also a good indication that Acer understood the market opportunity well and had planned its strategy accordingly. This was Acer's most important first step toward a successful business development.

Innovation Potential Assessment

For the internal innovation potential assessment, the following were considered:

- The ongoing projects
- Resources available in the company
- The corporate culture

The projects, resources, and culture were analyzed using the methods outlined in Chapter 6. The innovation potential maps for projects, resources, and culture were constructed and are shown in Figure 8-12. Everything was aligned for the projects innovation map except perhaps for the distinctive product innovation category, which is extra large. The reason for this was the personal emphasis by the company's management and professionals on development of products that could be stars and leaders; this caused a deviation from the strategy, which was to produce mostly followers.

For the resources innovation map, it was noted that resources had a medium level of capability in innovation of products of a breakthrough class. It was also noted that a small level of resources had breakthrough process innovation capability. On the positive side, this

Projects

	I	D	BT
P1	XL	XL	0
P2	L	L	0
P3	M	M	0

Resources

	I	D	BT
P1	XL	L	M
P2	L	M	S
P3	M	S	0

Culture

	I	D	BT
P1	XL	L	0
P2	L	M	0
P3	XL	L	0

Figure 8-12. Innovation maps for organizational assessment.

indicated that Acer was positioned for future development in the area of breakthroughs if the market opportunity and the corporation's strategy eventually called for breakthrough activities. On the negative side, this indicated a misfocusing of resources that was a drawback to business development, which depended on a focus on incremental and distinctive innovation. Since there was no project under breakthrough shown in the project innovation map, this resource capability probably created stress in the organization.

The organizational culture innovation map was aligned with the strategy. One observation was that distinctive innovation activity for both product and procedure were of a higher level than that for process, which was medium. This was probably due to the engineering- and marketing-oriented corporate culture of Acer.

These three innovation maps (projects, resources, and culture) were

Projects

	I	D	BT
P1	+1	+2	0
P2	0	+1	0
P3	−1	−2	0

Resources

	I	D	BT
P1	+1	+1	+2
P2	0	0	+1
P3	−1	−3	0

Culture

	I	D	BT
P1	+1	+1	0
P2	0	0	0
P3	+1	−1	0

Figure 8-13. Difference innovation maps for organizational development.

then compared with the strategy innovation map. The three difference maps were constructed as shown in Figure 8-13. A plus sign indicates that the innovation potential (whether it is in projects, resources, or culture) was higher than what the strategy called for. A minus sign indicates the opposite. Zero is ideal (aligned). A difference of 1 was not considered significant. A 2 or 3 was a warning that the innovation potential was not aligned with the strategy. A misalignment is a signal for the management to have action plans put in place to reduce the gap (the difference) between the internal innovation potential and the corporate strategy (which was aligned with the market opportunity).

The projects difference map indicates that there were misalignments in distinctive product innovation of + 2 and in distinctive procedure innovation of − 2. The + 2 is an indication that there were too many ongoing projects for products of a distinctive innovation class. The − 2 is an indication that there were not enough projects for procedures of a distinctive innovation class. The combination of these two misalignments points up the fact that the ongoing projects were initiated improperly in these two categories and should have been redirected.

The resources difference map also indicates that there were misalignments in the breakthrough product innovation category of + 2 and in the distinctive procedure innovation category of − 3. The + 2 is in line with the previous comment that too many resources had capabilities of breakthrough product innovations. The − 3 points out clearly that the resources were grossly inadequate to develop procedures of a distinctive innovation class. Again, it points out the fact that resources were misplaced and corrective actions were urgently required.

The misalignments indicated above, however, are not easily correctable. That is, Acer could not simply shift projects and resources from products to procedures, since they are of different nature and require different expertise (engineering in products and marketing in procedures, for example) to carry out their activities. Corrective actions (action plans) would involve

- Retraining (education)
- Transferring people (if they possess expertise in both engineering and marketing) while providing the proper incentive programs
- Restructuring of the organization in conjunction with the transferring of people
- Providing better communication systems and channels, so that the corporate strategy is clearly understood
- Improving management systems so that projects and resources are planned and put in place properly and consistently with the corporate strategy

The difference map for culture indicates that the corporate culture was in good alignment with the corporate strategy. This was highly desirable since if the two had not been in alignment changing the corporate culture would have been a very difficult and lengthy process. This alignment, however, was not an accident. Most of the people involved in the strategic planning were senior management and technical people who grew and matured with the company. These were the same people who had shaped and influenced the corporate culture during its formation and development.

Summary

The action plans described earlier were only a few of many actions taken by Acer which resulted in reduction of the gaps between the internal innovation potential and corporate strategy. Again, note that there was no market-driven innovation methodology available to Acer's management team at the time. These actions were taken due to sound management decisions by Acer. Had the methodology been available, its utilization would have enabled Acer management to make even better decisions with less uncertainty and guesswork. This case study of Acer shows how the market-driven innovation methodology could have been used to help Acer in the development of its five-year strategic plan as well as in the execution of the action plans.

When this case study was first finished in the summer of 1991, the results were presented to a team of top management people of Acer, many of whom were involved in the planning as well as execution of the five-year plan. They were impressed, and agreed with most of the interpretations of the case study. Furthermore, they were very enthusiastic in pointing out to us that while their company was successful in reducing the gaps between the strategy innovation map and the two internal innovation potential innovation maps (namely, projects and resources), their company failed at the time to realize that the same actions that reduced the gaps also tipped the balance and created a gap between the corporate strategy innovation map and the corporate culture innovation map. This gap gradually surfaced and represented a major concern to their company. Their company has been spending a great amount of time, effort, and resources to deal with this challenge. This methodology would have been very helpful in understanding how to develop the resources needed, refocus the resources to the strategy, and develop a strong, viable corporate culture.

9

Diversifying a Multinational Company

A New Business Venture of IBM

Observations

IBM's new business venture in computerized instrumentation, beginning in 1971, was extremely significant to the company. It demonstrated to IBM and its management team that different methods of doing business were possible before the need for large-scale change was recognized. It pioneered some of the business practices that were used later by the very successful IBM personal computer (PC) independent business unit. And now, many years later, some of the same lessons must be learned by thousands of IBMers as they try to figure out how to do business within the new IBM.

The first products of this new unit, which later became IBM Instruments, Inc., were not successful. The utilization of the market-driven innovation methods described in the earlier chapters clearly demonstrates why.

The strategy of the organization was driven by the personal vision of the fledgling entrepreneurs who made up the initial team. They were correctly focused on the need to demonstrate the viability of significant change to the business practices of IBM. However, they let this vision blind them to the opportunity in the market. To complicate matters even further, they were technology driven rather than market driven.

Another important factor leading to the failure of the first products was the schizophrenic culture of the organization, which had two diametrically opposed poles of culture. The organization was still part of IBM and had to fight to remove itself from IBM's culture. It finally became a wholly owned subsidiary of IBM eight years after its inception—long after the first products had been developed and marketed. This long-drawn-out battle for independence created a culture with both the old and new cultural elements present. This created a tremendous amount of stress within the organization, affecting its efficiency.

The combination of lowered efficiency as a result of fighting internal battles instead of being focused on the market, and poor effectiveness due to the improperly focused strategy, resulted in poor business results. Had our methodology been available to and followed by IBM, these problems could have been avoided and the early products been business successes. Perhaps, then, more attention would have been paid to the lessons learned and some of IBM's current malaise avoided.

Introduction

This is a retrospective case. IBM started this new business venture when it was very successful, and growing. In the early 1970s, IBM was interested in diversification and was experimenting with several diversification methods and markets. This case was developed and the analysis performed almost twenty years after the actual activity. It is a description of the first product developed and the market introduction of the new business venture. The case was developed through discussions with participants.

Case History

The Initial Task Force

A product development manager at IBM was asked to look into possible diversification opportunities. He gathered a group of engineers, managers, marketers, and finance people together. This small group of seven people was convinced that the bureaucracy and narrow product perspectives within their company were going to lead to severe problems in the future. They believed that if they could demonstrate in a small, internal, new business venture how to succeed without following the rules of the bureaucracy, they could affect the larger organization and save it from a disaster they saw coming in the future. The group was dedicated to the parent company and wanted to feel that they were accomplishing something of significance, and they were frustrated by their inability to facilitate significant change through normal channels.

At one point during the proposal process, several of the members sat in a room openly discussing what would become of them if the project were approved and funded. Future scenarios were outlined, and all of them ended with the originators being replaced by organizationally acceptable managers. In addition, they felt that they probably would not be rewarded. Unanimously, they agreed to go ahead anyway.

It became clear as the task force interacted with senior management that a significant business opportunity had to exist to attract attention. Markets with opportunities of less than $100 million were of little interest.

In reviewing past attempts at diversification, it became clear that, to succeed, the project had to

- Have a broad product line
- Be in a market area strategically important to the parent company
- Have some degree of autonomy (the more the better)
- Show some early results

The Initial Product Choice

After reviewing the potential of the market, the task force narrowed the range of opportunities to instrumentation; following additional market research segmenting that market into smaller categories, they selected analytical instrumentation as the niche market for entry. Guidance was given by senior executives in the parent company; the new business venture was to limit the entry to U.S. products and to make them stand-alone—not dependent on the parent company's products. This would avoid the entrapment of dependencies on IBM's established products.

After a search throughout the parent company, a set of technologies and applications were identified that would comprise the basis of a set of products of six different analytical instrument types. Hardware and software were available that allowed quick production of prototypes which demonstrated the reality of the project to the parent company and prospective customers. Soon after, external commitments were in place to field-test the prototypes. Application knowledge existed in the labs, plants, and sales branch offices of the parent company, and people were brought in from the parent company's development, manufacturing, marketing, sales, finance, and maintenance organizations. To minimize financial risk, a low-volume pilot production facility was established.

The choice of the first product family for the new venture was based on internal instrumentation capability, computational systems, marketing knowledge, and application knowledge. A fast-scanning spectrophotometer had been developed for an internal application, and this instrument was to be adapted to color measurement. There is a range of applications in color matching that require color measurement, and elaborate calculations based on those measurements. Applications in textiles, paint, plastics, glass, and even food processing require precise control of color. These applications seemed a natural test of the idea of application solutions (instrumentation, computer, and software), as they required sophisticated calculations and could be based on instrumentation knowledge already existing in the company.

The instrumentation technology for color analyzers seemed to have great potential for innovation. New methods of channeling the light through fiber optics both internal and external to the instrumentation were possible. This opened up possibilities of applications remote to the instrumentation itself and made the system less vulnerable to the environment. It also seemed possible to develop the ability to plug different types of measuring systems into the spectrophotometer. Different methods of scanning the visible spectrum were also on the horizon. While limiting resolution, fast-scanning techniques opened up other applications and, in general, increased measurement speed. In the future, all electronic-wavelength scanning looked promising.

Computer technology at the microprocessor level was just taking off commercially. The sky seemed to be the limit in on-board processing capabilities. A wide selection of displays were being developed, including flat-panel (e.g., gas panels) and liquid crystal types. Permanent and floppy disk storage devices were being developed in parallel for personal computers, as was all the rest of the digital technology.

Software and the application knowledge that it had to contain were at a rather rudimentary level. The basic theories had been developed for color matching in textiles, paints, and plastics many years ago, and were in the public domain. However, efficient programs that utilized these theories were not readily available in tested applications. Also, little had been done to tie the applications to business parameters.

In the basic application, say in textile color matching, the job of the system is to develop a formulation of dyes which, when applied to a fabric, will match the color of an arbitrary object presented to the machine. The samples to be matched can be of many different forms and shapes. The system must measure the color of the test object, then select a set of dyes and concentrations that will match the color of the test object. Since no set of dyes will exactly match the color, the job of the system is to pick several that come close, and then rank the match and cost to produce. The system can also keep other business data for the dyer.

Prospective customers of this type of product had been using trained people to do color matching. Through many years of experience, these people had developed skills that enabled them to match a sample given to them very closely. They were less able, however, to select the lowest-cost solution. Although there were competitive systems on the market, their makers had stuck to the old optical designs and just added computers. None of the competitors seemed very interested in innovating except by adding bigger or faster computers. The spectrophotometers were touted for their long history of accuracy and traceability to the National Bureau of Standards. The competitive measuring devices did not lend themselves well to remote measurements.

Both customers and competitors were willing and able to try new types of marketing approaches: rental, lease, or outright purchase plans were available. A "Try it, you'll like it" plan—where the customer gets the system for free for a short period of time—had not been offered by competitors, but customers seemed willing to experience this type of innovation in purchasing measurement systems.

Technologically, the systems were discrete-component systems. Each piece had been developed independently, and then all the pieces tied together. It seemed possible to innovate in the processes for integrated-circuit technology and automation, thereby reducing the overall cost remarkably. Customers for these systems were very cost sensitive. These customers functioned in an environment in which capital expenditures were limited. Investment in new technology was low; once capital was invested, payback had to be rapid.

There was also a certain amount of buyer reluctance among potential customers due to "FUD" (fear, uncertainty, and doubt). They had been using people to do the job for many years and had been getting by; they would have to be shown direct benefits in a nonthreatening way.

Unidentified potential customers did exist for the technology. Applications on-line in manufacturing and process situations seemed possible. Also, the number of precision color-matching applications for fast-scanning, microscopic color matching appeared large, if costs and application knowledge could be handled.

The current competitive systems seemed to meet their customers' needs, but few new customers had been added. The adoption of the technology was slow. New applications beyond standard color matching were only in the experimental stage, and only at the most advanced companies.

For the paint application, there was a structural competitor: customizing the paint at the dealer. Instead of offering premixed paint, a wide variety of potential colors are displayed and the customer picks the sample that best represents the color desired. The pigments are dispensed and the paint mixed for the customer. There appeared to be no structural competitors for the current textile application.

An Independent Business Unit Is Formed

Since the venture was intending to take advantage of a new business opportunity, the parent company management was willing to make procedural innovations to speed up entry into the market. An independent business unit was formed, which was charged with enthusiasm to innovate. They were determined to demonstrate to the host company and to the customers that they knew how to innovate effectively and how to get products to market fast. As a result, the units projects were all focused on integrating instrumentation technology with the newly emerging microprocessor and supporting technologies. Applications were chosen to take full advantage of this integration and of application-specific software. Novel instrumentation technologies with capabilities of extension to other applications were developed. An attempt was consciously made to significantly differentiate the unit's products from the existing competing products for the same application. The manufacture of the products employed rather conventional techniques. No significant attempt was made to lower manufacturing cost or improve quality through innovation in the manufacturing process. On the other hand, very significant attempts were made to develop very different procedures. New methods of purchase and lease were put in place. Sales and marketing were traditional except that international marketing with a very small group was started quite early. New methods revolutionary to the parent company were attempted in development, testing, and release to market.

The people of the organization were, for the most part, true believers in the vision. They primarily came from engineering and technical backgrounds and had little product development experience. They were brash and unafraid to test the limits of IBM's system, which they felt was creaking and groaning under its own weight.

The educational level of the people was high. Each person had had several different types of jobs, but most were limited to experience within the company. They had been with the company long enough to develop paradoxical views. They were well entrenched in the "company way," but perceptive enough to see the problems. They believed enough in IBM to want to change it from within, rather than leave, but they felt betrayed by the "system" when it began to attack them as they began attempts to change it.

The people in the group had many well-established contacts both inside and outside the company, and many external sources of information were used. Coincident with this, the leaders felt a real need to solve global problems internal to the company, but external to those they normally would have been expected to be solving. The lower-level person sometimes had trouble identifying with the global perspective.

The group's methods of communication were primarily verbal and factual. A few members, however, were quite able to represent ideas pictorially. Most of these people were willing to take risks. They had all left secure positions in order to make a difference. However, the group was very badly split in terms of thinking style. There were a number who thought segmentally, with a few of the leaders capable of integrative thinking. These were visionary people. The other members of the organization were concrete thinkers who primarily focused on things. As they thought mostly segmentally, they tended to view things as discrete objects which could be combined to result in some function. As a result, they tended to view their work in mechanical terms. The skills of the organization were predominantly focused on technologies leading to products.

The facilities of the organization—such as buildings, test beds (pilot lines), and classrooms—were predominantly focused on products, with some minor application to procedure. Equipment was almost all focused on product. The group was housed in a number of different buildings over the course of its history. Fortunately, the venture several times returned to an older building which had at one time been a research lab and therefore had much more of a "campus" feel than the traditional company buildings. The offices were all open to the environment, although their arrangement was very hierarchical. Each person, for the most part, had an individual office. The building had an auditorium and conference rooms readily available, and it even had a library. Recreation and exercise areas were available and open to all. The building sat in the beautiful old grounds of an estate, and walking was possible when weather permitted. A country club was available and accessible by a short car trip. Many members of the group participated together in team sports.

Pilot and manufacturing lines were one and the same. There were few procedures, however, and experimentation was possible. Manufacturing/pilot-line equipment was predominantly several generations old. Communication systems were state of the art for the time, and everyone had access to those systems. Test equipment was older, however, and laboratory equipment for this low-budget, start-up operation was not adequate. Design tools were either very primitive or nonexistent. Materials analysis equipment was not available in the organization; however, latest-generation analytical capability was available as a support capability from elsewhere in the parent company.

The intellectual property of the organization was formidable. The uniqueness of the designs and the focus on intellectual property gave the group competitive advantage. All patents and copyrights were focused on product. There were no trade secrets that it was necessary to guard. Know-how resulted in applications, procedures for operating within the company, software, and computer systems. There were no strategic relationships initially except with consultants, who advised only on products and procedures. This was recognized as a weak point and was eventually corrected many years into the program.

The organizational culture was a microculture inside a much larger and stronger culture. The microculture culture was predominately focused on products by the nature of the people, reinforced by the elements of the culture. However, inside both cultures, there was a strong focus on procedures. Inside the parent company's culture, the focus was on following procedures and creating new ones. Inside the microculture, it was on breaking with some procedures and simplifying others. The culture was predominately a "work hard/play hard" culture with a strong intermix of "bet your company." There was little "tough guy" and only slightly more process culture in the mix.

Opportunity Analysis

The opportunity analysis results are shown in Figure 9-1. It was clear from the analysis that the customer set was really interested only in incremental product innovations. There were existing systems that performed the function well enough; they had been proven technically over the years, and the technology had even been certified by the National Bureau of Standards. However, there were a number of potential customers for the equipment that were still using people for the color-matching task and didn't trust a machine. They needed new ways to get involved with the equipment such as trial usage, easy payments, and performance guarantees. Therefore, they were most interested in distinctive procedure innovation as there were few market and sales programs of that type available from the competition. Both current and potential customers really needed significantly lower priced equipment. Even though paybacks could be demonstrated of two years or less at an $80,000 price, capital was scarce in the textile industry. Breakthrough process innovations were therefore needed to resolve the cost problem.

The technology existed to allow these breakthrough product innovations. All the electronic and optical technology was converging synergistically to allow radically new equipment designs. The technological capability also existed for process innovations at all levels. The typical design of a spectrophotometer during this period involved discrete components which were assembled by hand. The technology was there to integrate the design to higher levels, thereby radically reducing the cost, although this, of course, would entail significant develop-

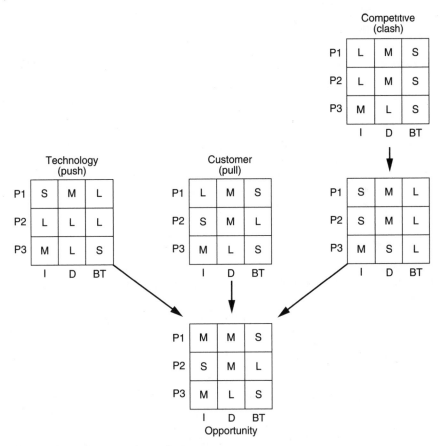

Figure 9-1. Opportunity analysis.

ment expense. The technology also existed to support the distinctive procedural innovation.

The competition, on the other hand, had adopted an incremental product strategy geared to meeting current customers' needs without expanding the market. Competitors had also adopted an incremental process strategy, and had invested little in improved manufacturing processes. The competition was active in distinctive procedural innovations. They were offering their products to customers in increasingly different ways.

Figure 9-1 summarizes this analysis of customers, competition, and technology. Note that the clash of competition is shown in two ways, as it is sometimes convenient to do. The first matrix represents the level of competitive activity. The second is a reversal of the first, thereby indicating opportunity for competitive differentiation.

The pull, push, and clash are summarized into the opportunity as shown in Figure 9-1. There are really no large product innovation opportunities. Customers wanted more initial product innovations, and the competition was responding. Even though there was technological capability for breakthrough, there was little if any customer interest. As a matter of fact, the industry was so conservative that they were suspicious of radical change.

The real opportunity lay in the process area. There was significant customer interest in much lower prices, and technological capability was there to provide it. In addition, the competition was ignoring this possibility. There was also some opportunity still in distinctive procedural innovations. There was customer demand, and even though there was competitive activity, there was still room for more.

Strategy

In this case, the strategy was determined primarily by the vision, mission, and goals that followed from the personal interests of the members of the organization. They were all technologists and drawn together by the technological capability. They drove toward breakthrough product innovations. The design of the spectrophotometer and the system were radically different than those of any on the market. There was very little manufacturing process capability in the group early in the design phase, so little attention was paid to that aspect of innovation. From a procedural standpoint, the organization's interest was primarily focused inward and was breakthrough oriented. They wanted to establish new business practices and procedures that would let them and other organizations within IBM operate more effectively.

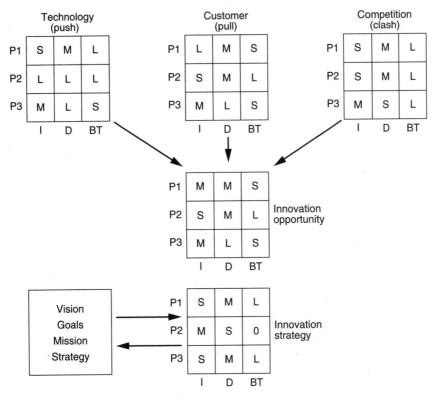

Figure 9-2. Strategy determination.

When the strategy is compared with the opportunity (see Figure 9-2), it can be seen that the strategy bore little resemblance to the opportunity. This was clearly a case of the requirements for the product, process, and procedure being driven primarily by an internal vision. It was tacitly assumed by the members of the organization that customers would catch the spirit of this vision and readily accept it. Likewise, it was assumed that the vision provided a significant competitive advantage.

Organizational Assessment

The projects of the organization were very much aligned with the strategy. The primary focus was on breakthrough products and procedures. Resources for the organization were heavily loaded toward products. There was no significant resource devoted to process innovations and only a small amount devoted to and capable of procedural innovations.

The culture was schizophrenic, mixing that of the parent company and that of the new business venture. As a result, the culture was at the same time incremental and breakthrough oriented. This caused significant problems in the day-to-day running of the organization, and the stress level was very high. This situation is summarized in Figure 9-3.

The comparison of the organizational assessment and the strategy is shown in Figure 9-4. The organization's projects were very much aligned with the vision-driven strategy but out of alignment with the opportunity. Resources needed significant improvement even to allow implementation of the process innovation strategy and were in no way adequate to allow the new venture to take advantage of the opportunity. Likewise, the resource capability was not there to implement the procedural innovation strategy. The culture needed to be more focused. In order to implement the strategy, the content of old culture of the parent organization needed to be reduced.

	Incremental	Distinctive	Breakthrough	
	S	M	L	Product
Projects	M	S	S	Process
	S	M	L	Procedure

	Incremental	Distinctive	Breakthrough	
	M	L	L	Product
Resources	O	O	O	Process
	O	S	S	Procedure

	Incremental	Distinctive	Breakthrough	
	L	M	L	Product
Culture	M	S	M	Process
	L	M	L	Procedure

Figure 9-3. Organizational assessment.

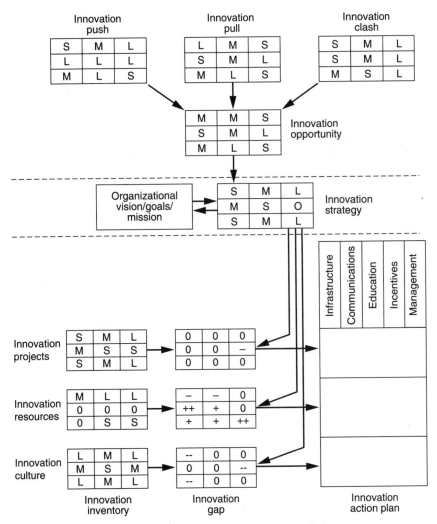

Figure 9-4. Comparison of organizational assessment and strategy.

Results

The first product of the venture was not very successful. It missed the market opportunity and there were considerable operational problems because of the lack of alignment between the innovation focus of the projects and the capabilities of the resources and the culture. There was frustration on all sides. The vision was driving the strategy, but it was not really meeting customer needs. As a result, the systems did not sell as well as expected, and each sale was expensive. The misalignment between the innovation content of the opportunity and strategy caused failure in the marketplace. The strategy and the organization's capability were not aligned, so there was considerable frustration because the vision was not being actualized, and misalignment of the projects, resources, and culture also caused frustration among the members of the organization.

The independent business unit, which later became the wholly owned subsidiary IBM Instruments Inc., continued to exist for a number of years after this first venture, which lasted for more than ten years. It had some successful products, but overall it was a business failure as measured in terms of financial return to the parent company. It was finally sold off after a long and futile attempt to diversify.

While not a glowing financial success, this venture was nevertheless of tremendous significance to the parent company. The "radicals" that founded it were right about the parent company's problems. The business practices they pioneered, using what is now called *process reengineering*, made it much easier for subsequent products closer to the parent company's mainstream to experiment. And, subsequently, the IBM PC generated billions of dollars in revenue for the parent company using business practices based on the venture's work. So, their vision was right for the company, just not right for the market.

10

The Seven Traits of Successful Organizations

What Are Traits?

As we have stated several times earlier in this book, culture is composed of philosophy, beliefs, values, behavior, and results. We have argued strongly throughout this book that an organization should be focused on innovation and managed by values, as an overlay to the traditional methods of management. Yet detection of values is difficult at best, and certainly requires probing of the organization with surveys, interviews, or examination of its documentation and results. It is sometimes easier to detect the underlying values by observing the organization's behavior.

There are several different types of behavior which can be observed. *Norms* of behavior are the patterns of behavior expected by the culture, and act as the base of the structure of behaviors. *Habits* are individual patterns of behavior which, if there is consistency among the individuals within the culture, can appear as habits of the organization. *Traits* are patterns of behavior that represent tendencies. Collectively, they produce an organization's characteristic mark or trace. Given an opportunity to react, how will the organization most likely respond? These patterns of behavior, collected over time, can be considered as traits.

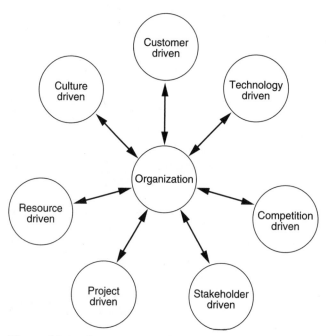

Figure 10-1. The seven traits of organizations.

The Seven Traits

It is our experience that all organizations have, to varying degrees, each of the seven traits we will discuss below (see Figure 10-1). And it is the variation of emphasis of these traits that gives a particular organization its distinguishing innovation profile. These traits also bias the innovation results of the organization. The variations come about as emphasis is placed on the trait, either by internal or external forces. It could be said that the organization becomes driven by the focus of its attention. This focus has then become the motivational force that energizes the organization.

Customer Driven

An organization that is customer driven focuses its innovation efforts to meet the needs of its customers. Embedded in this trait is the assumption that the organization understands the needs of its customers, which is not always the case. The kind of innovation that results will depend entirely on the type of customer the organization chooses to focus on. The feedback mechanisms will closely tie the organization and customer set together. Internal processes and procedures will be focused on the end customer as opposed to internal considerations. The measurements of the organization will be heavily loaded with customer satisfaction assessments. This type of organization is primarily reactive; it makes no move until the customer says so. In today's environment customer-driven organizations have a strong emphasis on traditional quality. They cherish the long-term relationships with their customers and this may even translate into personal friendships. Commonly, the management of the organization will come from a background of sales and marketing, internally promoted.

Service organizations are almost always customer driven. If they aren't, they will quickly lose their customers. However, if they are only customer driven, they will lose their customers to their competitors. The entertainment and food industries are also primarily customer driven. It is rare that one wants to go to an experimental restaurant, and entertainment becomes art as it moves away from being customer driven.

Suppliers of large organizations are customer driven. Many times their market is dominated by a single customer. They have grown up and with their customer, and they live, and unfortunately die, with that primary customer.

The innovation map of a customer-driven organization is flat. Any particular type of innovation is just as likely as any other type. It depends on the type of customer being satisfied (current, identified potential, or unidentified potential) and those customers' specific needs. Therefore, while there are specific innovation tendencies for individual customer-driven organizations, there is no general tendency.

Competition Driven

Competition-driven organizations are those that track carefully each move of their competitors and respond in like fashion. Their highest goal is to achieve the status of the "fast second." Acer grew from less than a $100 million to a $1 billion company and the largest computer manufacturer in Taiwan, with the strategy of being the best second. Organizations that are competitor driven are initially reactive. As they mature and reach an advanced stage of development of their strategy they become predictive, and they do an excellent job of tracking and predicting their, often multiple, competitors. Our surveys show that in general many Taiwanese companies employ heavily the tools of technology forecasting as most of the companies are either competition driven or technology driven. This is not surprising since the technology-forecasting tools are useful in either situation. These types of organizations have a strong focus on reduction in the time for product commercialization. The Taiwanese electronics companies have a product commercialization cycle that averages around nine months.

Competition-driven companies typically wait for someone else to develop the market before they make entry. They are typically managed by operations people, who keep constant pressure on getting the product out. Measurements emphasized are market share and cycle time. Good examples include consumer goods companies of all types; in particular, the soft drink companies, over-the-counter drug companies, and automobile companies are the epitomes of competitor-driven organizations.

The innovation profile of competition-driven organizations is flat across products, processes, and procedures. The activity focus will shift back and forth among these as the battle goes forward. However, there are differences in the class of innovations. Competition-driven organizations are not likely to produce breakthroughs; instead, they are much more likely to produce incremental and distinctive innovations. See Figure 10-2 for an example of a typical competition-driven innovation profile. The vertical axis indicates percent of relative innovation content.

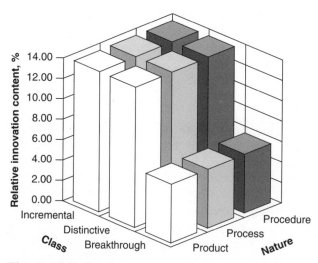

Figure 10-2. The innovation profile of a competition-driven organization.

Technology Driven

Technology-driven organizations are caught up in the "technology chase." As in the film and television series *The Paper Chase*, which depicted the pursuit of a law degree, the chase itself becomes the dominating driving force. The technology chase is an alluring quest. Technology is developed worldwide, and to enter into the technology chase is to compete in a global arena. However, the research and product development portions of an organization can easily drift away from the market in the technology chase. It is easy for them to start to consider the global technology competition instead of satisfying customers. They argue for competitive advantage based on technological innovation, and make compelling arguments. The quest is alluring because there seems to be endless potential in the technology. Technology appears to be able to solve every problem, and, each advance of the technology just serves as a spark to ignite the next stage of advance. Unfortunately, because technology follows the traditional S curve of advancement, as the technology reaches the saturation point, each new development costs more than the one before. That's when the real game begins, as the technologists then have to ask for more and more money to keep the game alive.

Technology-driven companies typically are either managed by a technical person, or else the R&D parts of the organization are very strong. R&D may even operate semi-autonomously. Because the organization needs money to fuel the technological development, and also to counterbalance the influence of the technologists, quite often these organizations have strong financial managers who can watch the money, and leverage its use. These organizations start out being very conscious of their technological competitors, but as they see more and more of their competitive advantage being built on the technology, they turn inward, they become insular, and also very security conscious. Since technological advance depends at least in part on information exchange, this is self-defeating, and accelerates the decline of the organization.

A classic example is the semiconductor industry. The industry started out with a great deal of openness. There was almost a free flow of technological information, as each company took great pride in being the one to announce at a conference or trade show the next advance. This was very good for the industry, and the world, as it facilitated the development of the industry and the applications built on it. There was a tremendous shakeout of the industry as those companies that could not convert the technology into products and cost effectively manufacture them lost out to those who could. Then the companies began to be more security conscious as each advance became worth so

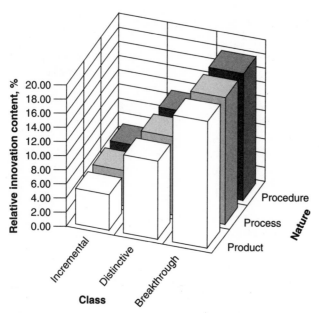

Figure 10-3. The innovation profile of a technology-driven organization.

much more money. In the meantime, the Japanese, who had benefited from the free technology transfer, had the freedom to build a new industry with a different basis of competition, and the U.S. companies began to lose out. In the early 1990s, the basis of competition is changing once again, with Taiwan and Korea as the newer competitors. The cost of advancing the state of the art in the advanced microprocessor area now exceeds $1 billion, and very few companies can play in this game.

The innovation profile of a typical technology-driven organization is shown in Figure 10-3. There would typically be a strong influence on breakthrough and distinctive innovations, mainly in the product area.

Stakeholder Driven

The nature and character of a stakeholder-driven organization vary depending on the type of stakeholder.

There are both internal and external stakeholders. Stakeholders—or, as one pundit called them, "snake holders"—can be the organization's employees, an individual visionary within the organization, the community within which the organization exists and operates, or the stockholders; they may be blends of both internal and external, such as labor unions.

External Stakeholders.   An institutional stockholder has different demands of the organization than an individual investor. Organizations driven by institutional stockholders typically invest a great deal of energy in making each quarterly income statement look good, since the price of the stock rises and falls depending on the investors' confidence in the organization. This drives a lot of short-term thinking within the organization, and influences the organization to institute an emphasis on innovation that reduces costs. A typical innovation profile would show a strength in incremental process and product innovations.

An individual investor typically would be a little more patient, although even this is changing in the United States as investors search for faster returns. However, they don't typically have the collective clout to influence companies that the institutional investors have. They would typically prefer to have the company invest more in distinctive innovations than the institutional investor, and in some cases are willing to invest in breakthroughs. This is especially true of the investors in privately held companies. Venture capitalists, business "angels," and private investors typically look more for the potentially higher rewards that come from the higher-risk breakthrough and distinctive innovations. They also would prefer to see tangible results of the innovations, so they look more for product innovations. They are rarely interested in process innovations unless they involve hardware or software. There is now a growing interest in procedural innovations as a significant return for service-oriented organizations has been shown.

Organizations can be strongly driven by the surrounding community as well. The organization's attention is totally on the needs and requirements of the surrounding community. Except in extreme cases, this is a short-lived phenomenon. Usually an issue arises in which the organization finds itself embroiled, and it must respond to the community in a timely fashion. However, counterexamples do exist. In Austin, Texas, for example, the real estate development organizations operating there are to a large extent captives of the strong community emphasis on environmental quality. These organizations must demonstrate their dedication to the environment before they can succeed in that community.

More traditional examples are organizations like the McNeil

Consumer Products Company, which dealt successfully with its Tylenol-brand tainted products. This situation has become a classic example of how to react to community pressure. On the other hand, Exxon and its unsuccessful dealings with the global community during and after the *Exxon Valdez* disaster provide the classic example of how *not* to deal with community pressure.

The innovation profile of the stakeholder-driven organization is typically strongest in the procedural area. The nature of community requirements will cause the organization to look toward breakthrough, or at least distinctive, innovations, particularly in the area of communications.

Another way of defining *community* is by looking at the regulatory arena, since regulatory systems operate in many environments and generally represent a greater community. Organizations operating in a heavily regulated environment often find themselves in highly reactive modes. A good example of this is the current regulatory environment for the pharmaceutical industry. The Federal Drug Administration has taken some very strong stances, and those organizations that wish to participate in the future of this industry must respond. Regulations appropriately conceived and written can actually incent innovations, but generally they act as inhibitors of innovations. This becomes a vicious cycle.

Two most interesting examples of regulation incenting innovation are the antitrust cases brought by the Justice Department against AT&T and IBM. In AT&T's situation, the company took advantage of the shifting environments to serve everyone's purposes, especially its own. Understanding that the efforts behind this response to the community were tremendous, and difficult to accomplish, the situation still afforded great opportunity for AT&T to innovate in all areas. Ultimately, this may prove to have been the opportunity of an organizational lifetime.

IBM's reaction on the other hand, was to fight the driving forces for change in an attempt to hold on to the past. They won their case and kept IBM together, only to have the driving forces prevail and tear it apart a few years later. When this happened, it actually caught IBM completely off guard. They had no time for planning, much less to gain control of the situation.

In addition, the fear of additional lawsuits and loss of the federal lawsuit constrained IBM's actions for a number of years and prevented its management from focusing on the market. As an example, in the early 1970s IBM considered many diversification activities. As part of one of them, the company considered an acquisition. Frank Cary, then CEO of IBM, would agree to the acquisition only if the internal entrepreneurs making the proposal could guarantee that no lawsuit would result. This acted as a block to this diversification.

Internal Stakeholders. Internal stakeholders can also drive organizations. Individual leaders with a personal vision of the future can drive an organization in an attempt to make that vision a reality. Sometimes this is in the best interest of the organization's customers and the organization itself, but more often than not it is detrimental. Unless the personal vision is created as a result of considering all the factors that are treated in this book, it will more than likely be developed in response to the individual's needs. The innovation profile of the individual visionary is, not surprisingly, breakthrough, perhaps distinctive; it is never incremental.

Employees can become strong stakeholder forces in extreme situations. Their impact on the organization and its innovation capabilities can be significant. In recent times several situations have developed in which the employees and their needs have overtaken the organization. These situations typically arise when an outside force is threatening the organization. Good examples of employees as stakeholders are Phillips Petroleum in Bartlesville, Oklahoma, and Apple Tree grocery stores in Texas. Phillips found itself several years ago fighting for its life during a takeover attempt. The employees reacted much like pioneers of the Oklahoma frontier—they circled the wagons, and became a mighty force that helped to fight off the attack. However, there was a great price to pay, and effects are still being felt today.

Apple Tree grocery stores are the employee-purchased stores bought from Safeway when that company announced its pullout from the Texas market. Initially, Apple Tree instituted a great number of incremental innovations, but as time went on they did not keep up with the pace of change.

Generally, the innovation profile of employee-driven organizations is high in the procedural area. They never get involved in the product area, and rarely become involved in process innovations.

Internal/External Stakeholders. An example of a blend of the internal and external driver is labor unions. They are composed of members of the organization, but have management which is outside the organization. In the past there have been many organizations in the United States that were labor union driven. This forced an emphasis on procedural innovations, quite often in the form of benefits and working conditions, which often inhibited other kinds of innovation. Enlightened labor leaders have now recognized this problem and are helping organizations focus on product and process innovations through the quality movement. But by and large labor unions are inhibitors of innovation.

Project Driven

Organizations that are project driven are dominated by the need to experience the sense of accomplishment that comes from successful completion of projects. Their projects involve very large and complex systems that take on a life of their own. Examples populate the federal laboratories, the space program, and organizations within very large companies. The completion of the task becomes the driving force for the organization, even if the project starts initially from a customer- or technology-driven focus. The superconducting supercollider project, until its cancellation, offered a good example of a project-driven organization. An excellent earlier example is NASA's efforts to put a man on the moon. The innovation profile is strongly breakthrough and distinctive, with an emphasis on product.

Resource Driven

Organizations that are resource driven quite often view themselves as being constrained. Resources (money, people, facilities, intellectual property, and strategic relationships) accumulated from past accomplishments need not be "boat anchors" to innovation; however, the organization must be willing to let go of the past if the past does not serve its innovation purposes today. This doesn't necessarily mean that the organization should rid itself of its resources. Resources are renewable and thus can continue to benefit the organization indefinitely. It is only when the mentality of the organization does not allow the resource to be changed, insisting instead on milking the resource of its value without investment in its future, that there are destructive consequences. In fact, the "cash cow" mentality is deadly in today's environment.

Quite often innovations in the ways the resources are used can drive the organization in very positive ways. For example, a small start-up company, low on money and short of people, can be innovative in its use of strategic relationships to grow both itself and its strategic partners.

A more traditional example of an organization that had the old perspective on resources is a company like Polaroid, with its introduction of instant movie film. This was not a technology-driven product; it was an intellectual-property-driven product, based on the internal capability of the organization. Xerox and Kodak are two other companies that have strong resource-driven organizations. As such, their tendency is to pay attention to their own intellectual property and facilities.

Organizations like the three named above place a great deal of emphasis on assessing their positions relative to "best practices" or "best of breed" measures. These benchmarking measurements are largely focused on and useful for organizations that are resource driven. This is a "mental bondage" problem; these organizations view themselves as constrained and therefore act in that manner. Whereas organizations that are competitor or technology driven use measurement tools associated with technology forecasting, resource-driven organizations make heavy use of benchmarking tools.

An extreme example of a resource-driven organization is a regional bank in Texas that is knowingly developing its entire business plan around a particular strategic relationship it has developed. This will unfortunately result in a decreased emphasis on its customers and its competitors, which in the long term will prove to be detrimental.

The innovation profile of the resource-driven organization shows predominately incremental process and product innovations. No large changes, which are associated with risks, are considered.

Culture Driven

Culture-driven organizations can have any type of innovation profile. It really depends on the culture. A company like Genentech has a breakthrough product orientation, whereas an organization like the federal government has an orientation to incremental procedure. When the organization is culture driven, it is a slave to its past. It has painstakingly developed the culture through trial and error to find the formula for success, and that culture is very difficult to change.

Culture-driven organizations can be very efficient when the culture is developed to optimize the organization's operation. When the culture is initially developed, it is also effective. The early culture matches the capabilities of the organization to the market, but as the environment changes the culture can get out of phase with the market, and then the organization will run into trouble. If attention has not been paid to the market for a long time, the culture will be vastly different than what is required, and there will not be enough time to make needed changes.

The culture of an organization can have a life of its own; in spite of many attempts to change it, it remains the same. The U.S. Postal Service is a good example of a culture- and resource-driven organization that has yielded very little to several attempts at change.

A recent article in the *Wall Street Journal* considered the negative side of education and training in companies. It discussed the fact that

IBM developed its culture very well. The company's culture was so well-defined, and the values of the company were so ingrained by its training and education, that it was very difficult to get it to respond, change when change was needed.

Dynamic Integration of the Traits: The Key to the Future

It must have become evident, as the seven traits have been described, that all organizations have each of them. Depending on the organization, one or perhaps two of the traits can dominate the focus of the organization such that it becomes driven by that trait.

Over the next decade, which spans the 1990s into the twenty-first century, it is completely clear that the organizations that will be successful will be innovative and market driven. A market-driven organization has a balance of the traits and is focused outwardly to its market. A metaphor for this type of balance is one of a bounded ecological system, such as a pond. The ecological balance of the pond is a highly interactive, dynamic one. There is constant change. However, if one force begins to dominate, the pond will eventually be doomed. Balance and change are the keys.

11

Delighting Your Customers

The Key to Business Success in the 1990s

Why Is Customer Satisfaction No Longer Satisfactory?

To prosper in the 1990s, companies must do more than just impress customers with *quality* and *efficiency*—the buzzwords of the 1980s. They'll have to go a step further, to *delight* customers with wonderful products, outstanding value, and superlative service. To move beyond satisfaction to delight, companies must be committed to constant innovation at all levels of the organization—in every department, not just research and development—and be market driven.

During the late 1980s, after decades of enchantment with sophisticated business school theory, U.S. management suddenly remembered that the element essential to their long-term success was continuing customer satisfaction. Once again they realized that fulfilling customer needs requires quality products, dependable service, and rapid response. This increased emphasis on satisfying the customer was certainly a step in the right direction. However, today's customers are no longer satisfied with just being satisfied. They have learned to take quality workmanship, timely delivery, and declining costs for granted. In the business environment of the 1990s, successful organizations will not be those that are content with developing merely satisfied customers; they will be the ones that commit to developing customers who are truly delighted!

The challenge is to understand the forces for change in the environment, and anticipate what innovations will appeal to customers even before the customers have articulated those needs. Genuine delight stems from giving a customer something wonderful that they didn't even know they wanted until they saw it. Then the company must create competitive production methods to develop—and hold on to—the dominant market share.

The people who first experienced the sound quality and convenience of the Sony Walkman were not just satisfied, they were delighted. People were not satisfied when they found that American Airlines would reward their business trips with free vacation flights, they were delighted. When people found that Federal Express would "absolutely, positively" assure next-day delivery, they were delighted, as were the people who found that they could take great pictures with little effort with their new electronic 35mm cameras. These are wonderful examples from the past. At the time that they were introduced, they indeed delighted customers. Today, when people purchase a portable music system they expect quality at least at the Walkman level. When people make airline reservations today they expect to get frequent flyer credit, and when they send a package out via an express delivery service, it is routinely expected to arrive the following day.

What delighted customers yesterday becomes today's floor, or basis for mere satisfaction. This is the real continuous improvement process which must be rigorously followed, for it results in improved effectiveness, whereas what today passes as "continuous improvement" only addresses improved efficiencies and never questions effectiveness.

Defining *Delight* in the Nineties

Would you rather be satisfied or delighted? Which do you think your customers would prefer? Chances are that you answered "Delighted" in both cases. The reason for this lies deep in the meanings of the two words. To be satisfied means to have desires and expectations filled. It literally means to have an end put to a desire, want, or need. Who really wants an end put to their desires? The word *satisfy* comes from the same root as *sad* and *sated*, which is what you become if you have all your desires satisfied.

To be delighted is to take joy or pleasure in something. The word has an element of surprise in it. To be delighted is to be provided with something that you may want or need, but not consciously perceive or expect. *Delighted* comes from the same root as *delicious* and *delectable,* words we associate with food. Wouldn't most of us rather have a delicious meal than one that merely satisfies our body's needs?

Delight comes from the same root as *lasso* which is what you will do if you delight your customers. You will be able to hold your current customers, gain a few more from the herd, and even capture a few strays from the range. And the customers that you delight will be enlightened by the product or service that you have given them. By surprising them and meeting their unrecognized needs, you will open their eyes to a range of possibilities hitherto unperceived by them.

To meet the unrecognized needs of your customers, you must be truly market driven. You must understand your customers, the environment in which they operate, what delights your customers' customers, the technological capabilities for solutions, and what your competitors are doing and likely to do in the future. You can delight your customers by helping them delight their customers more than your competitors do. To delight your customers requires innovation—market-driven innovation, not innovation driven by personal prejudices or desires, internal organizational needs, or technological capability.

Recognize that, to be successful, you must delight three different types of customers: current customers, identified potential customers, and unidentified potential customers. By delighting your current customers, delighting your competitors' customers, and delighting customers you didn't know you had, you are delighted! Wouldn't you rather be delighted than satisfied?

A Spectrum of Delight

Not only is delight a process, it is also a continuum; what delights one set of customers may not even be accepted by others, and may be actively rejected by still others. Which customer type you focus on to delight depends on your business strategy. Whether you are trying to hold on to market share, increase market share, or create new markets determines the focus of the organization's innovation activities, and consequently which customers get delighted.

Current Customers

Your current customers represent, to a large extent, a known quantity. You are probably well acquainted with their needs, operating styles, customers, suppliers, and competitors. You have established lines of communication, operating procedures, and feedback mechanisms.

Normally, these customers will give you the benefit of the doubt, and will continue to deal with you unless they are given a serious reason to terminate your relationship. On the other hand, the potential to grow market share with current customers is usually limited. If you look at the types of innovation that will be most likely to delight them, you will find that most often they will prefer relatively small improvements in your products and services—items which are a little better, a little cheaper, a little more reliable. These customers are normally well satisfied with your present products and services, and they will be delighted to see frequent and continuing improvements even if each one is of limited scope. Normally, they will not be particularly interested in major changes which will disrupt their present activities. The Gillette Company, for example, has dominated the safety razor market for more than six decades, not by revolutionary changes, but by regularly introducing limited product improvements.

Dangers exist. First, if you focus only on current customers, you are certain to lose market share in the long run because of attrition. Moreover, if you are too closely aligned to those customers, you face extreme danger. Go ask IBM. In a situation such as this, the customers become so close that they hesitate to be straightforward with you and tell you point blank that you are no longer relevant or do not innovative enough. They like you and they don't want to hurt your feelings, yet you've ceased to meet their needs. When they finally tell you it usually comes as a severe shock. And the switch from you to a new supplier is rapid indeed.

Identified Potential Customers

Your identified potential customers, on the other hand, represent an attractive opportunity for increased market share. Often, you will know, or can learn, almost as much about these organizations as about your own customers—the goods and services they provide, the markets they serve, their needs and requirements, and the firms they deal with to meet their needs. Unfortunately, they will usually have established relationships with your competitors similar to those you have with your customers. Normally, they will turn to you from their present suppliers only if you can provide them with a strong reason for doing so.

These customers will probably not be sufficiently impressed by small advances to switch from one supplier to another with the resulting disruption of established procedures and norms. To attract this group, you must offer a significant improvement over present products or services, in other words, distinctive innovations. As with your current customers, this group will not normally be intrigued by major (i.e., breakthrough) innovations, which can be very disruptive to their operations.

Unidentified Potential Customers

Your unidentified potential customers represent a way to expand a market or create a new market. To attract this group of customers, you must first make them aware of your product and service offerings; then you must entice them into making specific efforts to learn more about you. To accomplish this, you will probably have to offer products and services that are strikingly different from those being offered by others. Thus the innovations that are most likely to transform these people and organizations into new customers are those that offer something fundamentally different from the products and services presently provided by you or your competitors, that is, breakthrough innovations.

What Is a "Breakthrough"?

It is important to note that a breakthrough is defined by the customer. It is the customer's view of the innovation that determines its class, i.e., incremental, distinctive, or breakthrough. The personal computer (PC) represented a breakthrough innovation to individuals. It provided radical new ways of working and communicating. However, to the users of mainframe computers, in particular to information systems managers, the PC ultimately represented a threat. Information systems managers never viewed the PC as a breakthrough.

It doesn't stop here. Innovations in today's PC industry are clearly focused in all three areas—product, process, and procedure. However, most of the really interesting recent innovations have happened in procedures, specifically in marketing and sales. One of the truly delightful innovations to develop is the ability to call an "800" number, order your own PC over the phone and have it charged to your credit card, then have it shipped via Federal Express or U.P.S. directly to you. Individually, these procedures represented incremental innovations within the context of the marketing of consumer products; however, from the viewpoint of the PC customer they together represented a breakthrough in service. The context changed, and PCs were now in the same category as any item in an L.L. Bean catalogue. A series of incremental improvements within the same context can never lead to a breakthrough innovation; it is when the context is changed that a breakthrough can happen.

Delighting the Customer: An Example

Recently, two of the authors made a trip to Taipei, Taiwan, where they stayed at the Ritz Taipei for ten days. They were delighted by the experience, and were certainly lassoed, captured, and captivated by the hotel and its service. They will stay at the Ritz whenever they are in Taipei. Why is this so? The hotel is nice enough, and the facilities quite acceptable, but not even up to the standards of a business class motel in the United States. Yet the experience was much better than a stay at places with far more amenities. From the moment of check in to the time we left, there was a consistency of excellence in every interaction.

There were some nice innovations like unobtrusive but very effective computer technology for recordkeeping, and video cameras in all the halls that not only helped assure security but acted as a mechanism to alert the staff to check the room and clean it if necessary. There were many nice things like fruit every day in the room; a wonderful breakfast buffet; effective and efficient doormen who helped the poor Westerners get around without having to speak the language; fax capability that met communication needs; cool air conditioning individually controlled in the rooms that provided a haven from the heat and humidity; excellent soundproofing between the rooms, and, more importantly, insulating the rooms from the street sounds, which are considerable; and centralized controls of the room from the bedside.

Finally, there was the wonderful dinner hosted by the general manager, Mr. Patrick Su, for long-staying guests. It was a Chinese meal, which was most enjoyable. Mr. Su had arranged the dinner for twelve interesting businesspeople from all over the world; he skillfully led discussion and was very quick to pick up on any idea that might enhance a guest's stay.

Many hotels have these features and more. There are probably even other hotels in Taipei that do. The difference is that Mr. Su and the staff of the Ritz understand their customers very well, and they have created a set of innovations, an innovation profile, that anticipates and exactly matches the needs of the foreign business traveler to Taipei. Also, in every interaction with the hotel, its facilities, and its staff there is consistency. The staff anticipates needs so that in every transaction the constancy of purpose is evident.

Mr. Su understands how to delight customers. He understands the power of training, incentives, and measurements to get the behavior he wants. And he is a practitioner of values management. The values of the hotel are:

- Every staff member is the host on behalf of the hotel.

- We respect every guest's individual needs.
- We think ahead of our guests.
- Never say no!

It is these values which, together with the innovation pattern, delight the customers of the Ritz Taipei. A pattern of mostly incremental innovations, which are coupled together, and kept consistent with the values, is this organization's key to delight.

Essential Elements of Delight

Delight is a very simple concept, with profound strategic and tactical implications for organizations. There are only three essential elements:

- Anticipate customer needs.
- Fulfill customer needs.
- Be timely.

To anticipate customer needs an organization must understand the market. The market is composed of the driving forces for change, all customer sets, all types of competition, and all types of technology. The organization strives to understand both the present and future needs of all three types of customers as they are affected by the driving forces. Next, it is important to comprehend the power of technology to meet the developing needs or create new needs. Last, the competitive forces and how they are likely to act in the developing environment must be understood. For example, identified potential customers cannot be delighted without understanding future competitive capabilities and actions, since the organization's identified potential customers are currently its competitors' customers.

Internally, for organizations, developing the ability to anticipate customer needs requires that the organization literally have a "view" of the future. The importance of strategic thinking cannot be overemphasized. Strategic planners must be able to look as far out into the future as it will take for the organization to create the culture that enables the resources to be developed and the projects to be completed.

To fulfill customer needs, an organization must innovate to take advantage of the changes that are developing in the market. Innovation that takes advantage of change, rather than trying to cause change, not only meets developing customer requirements, it gains much faster acceptance. In a changing market many opportunities and threats will arise. The organization will be forced to choose which path to follow to take advantage of the opportunities and minimize or avoid the threats. The organization has at its disposal a continuum of strategies to create the path. The continuum of strategies is composed of a mix of the nine different types of innovations.

The organization must also be able to assess its own capabilities and develop additional capability, if needed, to effectively and efficiently implement the strategy it has chosen. Quality is one of the key components in fulfilling customer needs; however, quality must be defined by the customer, not by some internal or otherwise imposed quality program or standard.

To fulfill customer needs, the organization must have the capability of translating those needs into product specifications and manufacturing requirements. And in order to actually delight the customers, the members of the organization themselves must be delighted. As Donald E. Petersen, chairman and CEO of Ford Motor Company, so eloquently stated,

> To go that extra step that builds a competitive edge, we must learn to delight the customer, as was once suggested by Colby Chandler, the chairman of Eastman Kodak. We need to inspire the customer's total emotional response. To do that, the company must generate a positive emotional force from within, a force that can come only from its people. They must be stimulated and supported by constancy of purpose on the part of their leadership; by true delegation of authority to those who must perform the task; by a passion for quality throughout the company; and by encouragement, reward, and opportunities for learning. I am convinced that the passion of the employees begets the passion of the customer. Companies can capture their employees' emotional involvement. What we're learning at Ford is that no enterprise can provide more quality to its customers than it provides to its employees.[1]

To be timely in the market is to understand the window of opportunity, and to be there with the innovation. If the innovation is introduced too early, it will not gain acceptance. If the innovation is introduced too late, either your competitors will already have captured a significant share of the market, or the needs will have changed and your innovation will no longer fit. The common metaphor used here, "the window of opportunity," is very appropriate. In delighting the customer, timing is everything. But the ability to be timely in the marketplace seems elusive to many organizations, and to many others timeliness of an innovation is due to mere happenstance.

In order for an organization to be consistently timely, it must be efficient in translating its collective knowledge about the market into specific actions that are meaningful to customers. This means that all internal systems are synchronous and yet are able to be flexible enough to dynamically respond to the changing needs of the market and to internal problems. Timeliness implies being able to translate the strategy into implementation plans, having a sufficient number of significant measurements, and having the management capability to manage to the plan.

The Quest to Become Truly Market Driven

Innovation is a process. But, it is no longer a mechanical process, just as organizations are no longer accurately described by mechanical metaphors. Unfortunately, our language and tools have yet to catch up with needs for describing these dramatic changes in thoughts and concepts. What we have described in this book is only an approximation to what should go on in an organization. What we have described in the form of linear processes are really dynamic, interactive, and organic. It is the linking of the market to the culture through the strategy and capabilities of the organization by the means of innovation and its underlying values that is imperative to success in the later half of this decade and beyond.

As a process, its metaphor in the organization is a quest. Like all quests there are discoveries, obstacles to be overcome, disappointments, changes in direction, help from unexpected sources, and enlightenments. It is always an adventure and it will be transformational. Your quest must be uniquely yours. Each market and organization is slightly different and hence demands a different approach. But they can all, in our experience, be handled by the structure and concepts described in this book. There is an old saying about life: "Walker, there is no path. You make the path by walking." This is also true for developing innovation in organizations. Now it is time for you to start walking and helping your organization along that path to more market-driven innovation.

Reference

1. Donald E. Petersen, "Creating Customer Satisfaction," The Conference Board, New York, May 29, 1990.

Index

About the Authors

PAUL A. SCHUMANN, Jr. is a founder and president of Glocal Vantage, Inc., an Austin, Texas-based business development consulting firm. Mr. Schumann is a recognized expert in corporate growth strategies and organizational development.

DONNA C. L. PRESTWOOD, a founder and vice president of Glocal Vantage, Inc., has been a corporate growth specialist for nearly twenty years, serving some of the largest companies in North America and Europe as a consultant, project manager, speaker, and lecturer.

ALVIN H. TONG, a founder of Glocal Vantage, Inc., is internationally known for his expertise in science-based parks and has served as a consultant to science parks in Taiwan, China, Malaysia, and Vietnam.

JOHN H. VANSTON, president of Technology Futures, Inc., has been actively involved in the management of technology innovation for more than two decades.